THE REVENUE
CATALYST
MASTERING THE ART OF SALES

Leaders
Press

GEOFFREY M. REID

POWERFUL STRATEGIES FOR EXPLOSIVE GROWTH
AND PREDICTIVE SUCCESS IN B2B AND B2C SALES

Leaders
Press

ISBN **978-1-63735-279-3** (pbk)

ISBN **978-1-63735-280-9** (hcv)

ISBN **978-1-63735-281-6** (ebook)

Library of Congress Control Number: **2024900984**

Praise

Geoffrey M. Reid's The Revenue Catalyst turns the art of selling into a science of winning!

Dr. Aaron Poynton | CEO, Omnipoynt Solutions and USA Today & WSJ Best Selling Author

Geoffrey expertly combines the science, art, and attitude of sales to create a comprehensive guide for business leaders looking to maximize revenue. He goes above and beyond sharing sales techniques. Through a strategic approach focusing on team development, market understanding, and company structure, Geoffrey offers the practical tools required to develop people and processes, and ultimately drive performance. The Revenue Catalyst is a valuable resource for any organization looking to build a culture of sales and remain competitive amidst shifting market conditions

Samantha Kris | Certified Reinvention Practitioner, Acclaimed Speaker & Best-Selling Author

In *The Revenue Catalyst*, Geoffrey Reid offers clear, actionable insights that stand out in the crowded sales landscape. A must-read for sales professionals.

Jody DelVecchio | Director, McLean & Company

The section on high probability prospecting is a keep and fit for salespeople looking to target the right leads, with a valuable guidance on infusing strong mental attitudes into sales culture, a crucial aspect often overlooked.

Martin Treis | Senior Business Partner Manager, Smart Bridges GmbH

I was fortunate to receive an advance copy of Geoffrey M. Reid's insightful book, The Revenue Catalyst. This book reveals the essential role of sales in driving organisational success. Through practical strategies and valuable insights, Reid empowers professionals to elevate their sales game, essential for career growth in today's competitive landscape.

Kumar R Parakala | Founder and President, GHD Digital, Entrepreneur and Board Director

Geoffrey Reid delivers a masterclass in sales strategy, offering a holistic approach to sales that transcends industry boundaries, and providing sales strategy that drives tangible results.

Joe Alpark | Chairman / Director, DFO

The Revenue Catalyst provides advice on negotiation strategy, essential for closing deals effectively in today's competitive market. Not only that, but it also shares important insights about making sales predictable with data and offers practical tips for benchmarking performance and achieving consistent results.

Douglas Ferguson | CEO & Founder, Cyberseconomics

As a seasoned sales professional, I can confidently say that The Revenue Catalyst by Geoffrey M. Reid is the most comprehensive and actionable guide I've ever come across. Prepare to be amazed!

Carl Grant III | CEO, Capital Raise

Geoffrey Reid's exceptional storytelling in this book makes sales strategies not just accessible, but engaging. His background as a teacher shines through every chapter, transforming complex concepts into lessons that are both clear and memorable. A must-read for anyone looking to master the art of sales.

Draga Sfetsios | Director, Marcus Evans

Geoffrey Reid debunks misconceptions around sales by providing a teachable process to implement sustainable yet adaptive sales strategies. His book offers insightful guidance and indispensable tools that can be taught, replicated and scaled to generate predictable results. A must-read for anyone serious about sales!

Chris Hebert | Treasurer, DFO

Geoffrey M. Reid's The Revenue Catalyst is a must-read for anyone serious about mastering the art of sales. Whether you're navigating the complexities of B2B or driving consumer engagement in B2C, Reid's insights provide a powerful toolkit for explosive growth and sustained success. This book is not just about closing deals—it's about building a sales culture that thrives on precision, adaptability, and relentless pursuit of excellence. With practical strategies and real-world examples, Reid transforms sales from a transactional exchange into a transformative journey, making The Revenue Catalyst an essential guide for today's sales professionals.

Rami El Arja | Chief Administration Officer

Throughout my extensive sales career, Geoffrey M. Reid stands out as the best mentor I've ever had. His unparalleled ability to break down complex concepts into easily digestible insights is truly remarkable. This book provides readers with a comprehensive guide that not only challenges conventional wisdom but also addresses the gaps left by traditional business education. Covering everything from the psychology of sales and effective team development to leveraging data and KPIs for predictable outcomes, this book is an invaluable resource for anyone looking to excel in the field.

Steve Ferris | Strategic Sales Executive, ConnectWise

If you're looking for a sales book that is one of your typical, work less, get rich quick, buy a Lamborghini, and Instagram influencer rags... Then this book isn't for you. If you're a sales professional looking to develop and sharpen processes, structures, and concepts that have been developed by the Chief Executive of one of the most successful events companies in the world, then read on. I met Geoffrey Reid at 22 years old straight out of University with little to no business experience. Within 6 months I was cold calling C-suite executives from some of the largest corporations in North America and closing deals on a 24-48 hour timeline. I had a phone, a script, and daily sales training with Geoff, that's it. Fast forward 14 years later as a serial entrepreneur, I will still tell you the most valuable professional and personal experience were those months spent with Geoff. I have since leveraged all of those skill sets and applied them to each company I have started and exited since. My first start-up out of Marcus Evans, we implemented the exact same sales processes and generated over a million dollars in sales within the first quarter selling a first-of-its-kind experiential marketing product to Canada's largest media buyers and creative agencies. Despite the emergence of AI and automated marketing SAAS type of products, the art of the sale will always be mastering the art of communication and the many complexities and layers that come along with connecting with another human being. If you want to learn how to close large deals with top decision-makers... Turn the page.

Paul Reynolds | Co-Founder/President, Skiprock

The Revenue Catalyst provides the blueprint and essential frameworks that organizations need to create predictable revenue streams with their sales team.

Graham Collie | Vice President, Aylo

Some people may misunderstand that sales is not just about talking and selling. I recommend this book so that they will read Reid's insights on leveraging data and KPIs to enhance sales predictability.

Ian Braganza | General Manager, Valnet Inc.

Geoffrey's book is a comprehensive guide for aspiring entrepreneurs but also for people who want to truly break down the various pieces to the jigsaw needed to elevate their sales skills.

Andrew Mowat | Director, Corporate Legal Advisors Group

I had the privilege of working with Geoffrey for 11 years. During this time, he was not just my boss but also a mentor, a friend, and an elder brother. Together, we engaged in countless discussions, forged strategies to drive sales, and faced disagreements along the way. We shared numerous dinners, lunches, and phone calls. We celebrated many victories, endured a few losses, and through it all, I became a true disciple of his work.

Now, the world has the opportunity to learn from his wisdom through this book—a chance to embrace a different approach to sales and elevate their sales acumen, provided they implement his teachings. Unfortunately, they may not get to experience the privilege of working directly under his guidance as I did, but his insights, especially on "Resistance selling" and the psychology of sales, are unparalleled. These concepts are presented with a level of class and emotional intelligence that is rare in sales literature.

I am proud to be a student of Geoffrey Reid. His influence is woven into all my interactions—whether with colleagues, new sales professionals, my family, or in other areas of my life. His legacy lives on through his work and through those of us who were fortunate enough to learn from him.

Khalif Samuels | General Manager, Marcus Evans

I dedicate this book to my father, Alan D. Reid K.C., whose guidance, inspiration, and example, through the writing and publishing of his own books and music, have helped ignite my desire to do the same. After having first learned from him at the age of fourteen how to write a high school essay, and subsequently undergraduate and graduate-quality work, he has also played an important role making this book at reality.

Nevertheless, this valuable skill set represents only a small part of what I have ultimately learned from my parents, including my mother, Barbara, perhaps most importantly, how to love, care, and think properly. I love you both!

I am also very appreciative to Marcus Evans, whose influence has profoundly shaped my understanding of business. By founding the remarkable company where I first learned sales, and later granting me the privilege of working closely with him, I am fortunate to have had such an experience while gaining invaluable knowledge. I am also grateful to Theron Burraway, whose exceptional sales acumen has left an indelible mark on me.

Furthermore, none of this would have been possible without the collaboration of dozens of incredible sales and business innovators, who I have had an opportunity to both mentor and learn from over the last nearly quarter-century, while at the same time becoming dear friends. It has been most satisfying observing wonderful people come up through the ranks internally to become some of the very best at sales I've ever observed, or on occasion go on after to use similar methodologies in other fields of business while finding further professional success.

Many thanks to Tom, Natasha, Andrew, Khalif, Marc, Draga, Kevin, Les, Alex, Mike, Steve, Michael, Graham, Steve, Pascal, Gus, Deborah, Jody, Courtney, Taina, Louisa, Lyne, Joe, Paul, Chris, and all the others who have contributed to this shared journey of growth and achievement.

Table of Contents

Foreword

In 2001, I advanced from a role that was nowhere near suitable to what I felt was my intellect, which was mostly ego framed in self-entitlement. As a very young man, I was asked to interview for a role at Marcus Evans. When I was hired, I learned quickly that it was a hard day's work sitting at a desk, needing to exchange those eight-hour days into hundreds of phone call minutes as was compulsory, in addition to a very high number of mandatory "dials" out.

Using the old-fashioned continuous computer paper that folded back and forth, we printed out "leads" for the day from a relic of a website that we purchased an account on that (at that time) was permitted to give private information of CEOs and other officers of companies as that was the law if they were publicly traded. But I digress.

The tonality that was needed for those early cold call discussions was similar to that of a world-class therapist, mixed with Wall Street brokers. After shifting from team to team within the various products of the company, I landed on the team of Geoffrey Reid. The quiet, Jedi-like demeanor. Short ginger hair and neatly trimmed beard.

Every word had a slight stutter that was not a result of any physical need but an internal assurance that every word was positioned and conveyed with absolute precision and relevance. If a wrong message was uttered, it was corrected within the blink of an eye. Geoff had a hardwired mechanism that ensured that he never gave the wrong signal, message, or utterance of data. There was no time for miscommunication. His mind was constantly working. When you spoke to explain a challenge or issue or if simply working something out for some strategic path, he would listen intently, never distracted, always nodding gently and waiting to calculate that information to respond with (what I always assumed his brain mechanisms were) a four-digit percentile correctness in his solution.

I remember countless times that I would hand the phone over or have him call a client back that was on the verge of making a final decision on sponsoring one of our summits at quite a high price point. There were, admittedly, times when I could have easily closed the sale, alone, to the point that they would nearly beg to sponsor and I would still hand the phone to Geoff. The reason was simple as it was for everyone else that did this with Geoffrey Reid: to watch this Shakespearean play, this Demosthenes-meets-Lincoln-meets-Dr. King massaging the brain of the client and, to be fair, those who watched this ballet.

Every word made sense. Every single feature and benefit was orchestrated into science. I would listen and realize every item that I had missed in my conversations that made perfect sense of inclusion in that particular event. It was breathtaking to watch. This was daily. It was pure joy and worth the long, arduous hours of fatiguing sales calls.

At the pub, after work, I'd recite these calls like I was some bard regaling the victories of Achilles, Odysseus, and Beowulf. I learned as much as I could, but the best I could do was attempt to understand the top-line disciplines of each sales conversation.

Over the two decades past this, Geoff had quietly mastered psychology and intuition like a monk sat on a mountaintop for some millennia. Geoff understood that the essence of sales lies in the fusion of psychology and intuition—the delicate balance of science and artistry. He knew, early on, that it was guided by the principles of psychology that needed the decoding of the intricacies of human behavior while that intuition. which he had in plenty, provided insights beyond the realm of predetermined logic. Together, they transcend mere transactions.

In this trademarked Geoffrey Reid dance of commerce, salesmanship becomes a profound act of understanding, empathy, and influence, elevating it from a transactional exchange to a transformative journey to which we all learned from and though our professional paths have diverged, his lessons continue to resonate, guiding me through the ever-evolving landscape of my career.

I can promise you that through his words in this book, you will discover that he has far more to offer than I have ever had the presence to understand.

Michael MacLennan
Founder of Sonas Event Management

Introduction

Business schools have a problem: Most, if not all, of them neglect sales education. They focus only on four disciplines: finance, accounting, marketing, and human resources. This has created widespread misunderstanding of sales as a broad field. It has also led to CEOs and other executives failing to understand the full potential of sales, while generating revenue for their companies remains their main challenge.

I'm sometimes asked why I think the study of sales is neglected in business schools. How I answer the question can be gleaned from a discussion I had with Dr. Alan Shepard, the president of Concordia University in Montreal, Canada, where I formerly taught and studied.

It was late February 2019, and I was working out of our corporate headquarters in London. Shepard and the university's VP of advancement, Paul Chesser, were in the UK visiting alumni, former professors, and other members of the Concordia University community based in London. It was his farewell tour because, at the end of the year, he was taking up the post of president of the University of Western Ontario, which is another prestigious university in Canada.

I remember him sitting in my office with his colleague and asking me, "How are we doing in terms of supplying students that are well-educated and prepared to contribute to your company?"

I replied, "Quite well, since I have hired a lot of successful employees who graduated from Concordia and also from JMSB [the John Molson School of Business, which is Concordia's business school]."

I then asked, "But why is there so little sales education? This is not just at JMSB, since a lot of other business schools

I hire from seem to share this same gap in sales education. Across the board, there only ever seem to be four disciplines at most business schools: finance, accounting, marketing, and human resources. Why is this? Whatever happened to the fifth discipline?"

That fifth discipline, sales, is what most CEOs are responsible for—more often than not, revenue is more important for them to grow than other aspects of business.

Shepard laughed and said, "Well, most professors just aren't comfortable teaching things that they don't know enough about."

I thought it was a pretty profound quote at the time, and it led me to informally ask many of the business students I would interview afterward whether they had taken sales at a university. Sometimes someone would say that they had taken one class that was available when they were an undergraduate or in their business degree. Most of them said none.

This book provides the fundamentals that any student would need to learn if they were attending a business school that focused on sales. In the following pages, you will learn how product positioning helps give weight to a sales strategy. You will get an overview of how to create a sales process that's in line with your positioning strategy. I'll also show you how to select and develop a high-performance sales team and how to boost the predictability of the sales process by using data and key performance indicators (KPIs).

Like any other discipline, sales strategy has evolved over time, and this book will explain what this means to modern sales practitioners. We also delve into the tactics and techniques of effective salespeople, including

- ❖ prospecting;
- ❖ online outreach strategies;
- ❖ negotiating;

❖ the concepts of resistance and indifference as they apply to sales; and

❖ the importance of time management.

Additionally, we'll take a look at what constitutes a good lead and how to optimize your prospecting efforts.

To succeed in sales, it helps to develop a positive mental attitude. We'll discuss the science of how the brain is wired, how to stay positive and use "flow" to improve results.

Process tools are also vital to sales success, so we'll explore techniques for structuring and delivering a pitch, asking the right questions, and handling whatever objections a potential customer might make. This book concludes with an in-depth look at becoming an effective closer: how to prepare for the close by asking carefully calibrated questions and how to effectively use objections and hypotheticals when closing sales.

So how did I get here?

My background was not in sales. I'm more of an academic who had done a lot of university study before later being hired as an adjunct professor teaching conflict resolution, mediation, and negotiation in the School of Graduate Studies at Concordia University in Montreal, Canada. However, it was my unique experience in the emerging field of modern mediation, which I acquired immediately after my education, that qualified me for my appointment as a professor and teaching those disciplines for five years.

Before that, I had been working in the public sector in several different roles. Then I got an opportunity to partner with notable people in the field of mediation, negotiation, training. This led to the creation of an interdisciplinary alternative dispute resolution (ADR) center for problem-solving, which gave me an opportunity to exchange services for money. That happened early in my career. It was an interesting exercise with lots of potential because we had excellent people, the timing was right, the market conditions were right, and we had a phenomenal opportunity.

It was an emerging field—this was in the mid-1990s before the legal industry in the years following gradually took over the modern mediation movement—and it seemed like everyone was looking for some type of mediation services or other services using collaborative process strategies. There was a real need for mediation, training, and consulting, whether to help individuals resolve conflicts, for companies to reduce incidents of harassment and other forms of liability, or for governments to use collaborative processes to implement regulations or design public policy that people would comply with voluntarily. It was an exciting time in my professional evolution, but at the time I still didn't know the first thing about sales.

I didn't know how people in business generate revenue. Do they reply to an RFP (request for proposal)? Do they obligate people to buy from them? Do they work their contacts or Rolodex? How do you go out and drum up business?

These questions led me to a place where I was transitioning to the next phase of my career after a few years in this field. I realized that I was going to have to put a lot of work into generating fresh clients for the business if I wanted it to grow.

I was thinking, *Well, how do I do that better this time around?* I had two choices. One was to just continue doing the traditional management consulting/mediation/negotiation /training, whether or not it was my own business. The other option was to fix the gap in my skill set, which was a complete lack of understanding of sales.

I chose the latter, and I went out into the market looking for the best sales experience I could find. It was an interesting exercise because I was doing a lot of research and talking to a lot of people, and I just happened to stumble upon a global business events company. That company, which was later rebranded the Marcus Evans Group, was already renowned for having very specific sales structures as well as excellent new hire sales training. So I opted for that particular exercise. I was both consulting and teaching graduate school at university at the time. As a consultant, I went from charging a generous per diem fee for my services to a low base salary in sales but with the promise of high commissions for results and revenue generated. In retrospect, there were risks, and I arguably took a little bit of a step backward to try to acquire a skill set that I knew nothing about.

It turned out that, with all the other knowledge I had, I just happened to be good at selling. At the end of my first full year with the company, I was the top salesperson in North America in terms of new revenue generation. This success, combined with my other skills, helped me to start rising through the management structure of the organization to eventually become a chief executive. Ultimately, the expertise in sales I developed stemmed from a choice that I made—because I could have gone in a completely different direction. I think it shows figuring out what we don't know and trying to fill gaps and rounding out our repertoire can bring great opportunities,

How a lack of sales training impacts the ability of business students to succeed in the workplace depends on the type of organization they join. Many companies have a sales program for their new hires, in which they teach them a certain methodology. Sometimes those methodologies are really strong, sometimes they're not. What I've discovered through coaching CEOs of firms that do business-to-business sales is that there isn't a uniform approach to sales.

There's an interesting comparison that I like to use. I describe sales as being a big tent, since there are a lot of methods called "sales" that are very different from one another. And how people tend to sell is really a byproduct of how children learn to get things when they're kids. The only way you can actually have an impact on your parents giving you things is by being *persuasive*:

"Come on, Mom. Buy me the sugar cereal at the supermarket. We're going to eat it together. It's going to taste great. Come on, let's buy it. Let's do it."

Then children become teenagers, and it's about influencing their friends: "Let's go here. Let's go there. Let's do this as well. Come on, let's do it."

All this is persuasion.

Then some of them go to business school where they don't get a sales education, and they come out into the real world where they lack sales tools, so the only thing they really know how to do is to push and put pressure and do things in a way that is often not well received.

I've interviewed two thousand or more candidates in my career in hiring for sales positions, and it's very rare that someone has an intuitive understanding of how to approach the job, aside from using the persuasion strategy.

Neglecting sales in business education impacts the bottom line. I think there are a lot of businesses that underperform and don't get off the ground because a business is often only as good as its weakest component. If a company doesn't have a great sales strategy or sales organization or isn't able to develop sales leaders and really ensure that people are making informed decisions, it's likely to impede the organization's success.

If sales isn't made into an organization's strongest component, money will always be left on the table. In fact, many businesses with terrible products but great sales end up generating a lot of money (although that is unlikely to be a sustainable business model).

That's where you read about people cashing out on things because they have a fabulous sales strategy but, arguably, a weak product or something that just doesn't stand the test of time. Some people will go from one product like that to another, selling all their lives because the sales skills that they have are always going to be able to create revenue out of thin air.

That's essentially what sales does—it creates money out of virtually nothing, based on the ability to engage with people. A lot of the time, customers don't know why they buy, and being able to shape what they buy through smart questioning is entirely possible. That's why sales works.

I can say to someone, "Hey, some of our friends are going to the lake this weekend. Would you want to come?"

Or I could say, "Some of our friends are going to the lake this weekend. You wouldn't want to come, would you?"

Typically, one would be more inclined to want to come when a question is charged negatively because people's emotions cause them to desire and value more things they can't have. Just by charging a question, positively or negatively, you create either an absence or a different type of conclusion.

I'll get into more detail on these techniques later in the book, including smart questioning and how good habits or bad habits are sticky, which relates to sales and why sales works.

The book will also explore the challenge of choosing the right types of salespeople. Is it just about hiring someone with a Rolodex and a deep contact list? Or is it about giving people the tools to tap a broad understanding of sales so that they can help shape the positioning to make it easier for them to utilize sales skills other than guilt or obligation? Or is it more about a commitment to give people with the right attitude sales process training, which is fundamentally negotiation training?

Much of sales comes down to specific skills. For instance, you need to be able to recognize what question is needed in any given situation and inject it into the conversation to uncover the most information. That makes the difference between the sale being merely transactional (where the salesperson is basically just taking the order) as opposed to being transformative (getting prospective customers to realize how the product or service will benefit them).

Students also need to learn about handling objections. How do you take challenging issues and turn them into advantages? How do we structure pitch presentations and lay out information in a sequential way that allows a potential customer to connect emotionally and react to it positively? How do we create fertile conditions to elicit a yes and how do we avoid inadvertently nudging customers to say no? How do we structure closing questions, and how does that serve us?

I don't think there is a consensus on what best practice effectively or fully taps into what's available.

To learn the most important skills of a salesperson, people almost have to unlearn how they have been able to push and persuade in the past. Putting someone through the wringer, or just being pushy and abrasive and relentless, has effects that are counter to sustainability in sales. Unfortunately, that tends to be what people often come to the table with, and they think that they have to do that to show that they're confident or assertive—that's their only tool, their only weapon, and they need to learn to refrain from pushing on a rope, so to speak.

It's much better to create a vacuum that propels prospects' desire to buy toward you, or sometimes, as I describe it, "leaving the breadcrumbs for prospects to follow."

Perhaps the number-1 thing that gives sales a bad reputation is when it's obvious that salespeople are pushing an agenda for self-interested reasons as opposed to what is in the collective interest, i.e. "win/win" or for reasons that are in the client's interest

Doing sales in that way is, arguably, not sustainable and, in my view, represents a mere fraction of what's actually possible. There is a whole retinue of brilliant process techniques that can be used to create a transformative experience in someone's mind so that by the end of a conversation, they're seeing and doing things very differently than they were at the beginning of the conversation. That's because they've been stimulated by processes that bring them through a long thought process and almost make it their idea at the end.

Over time, as in any area, there's been an evolution in terms of how people buy and how people sell. If you look back, there have been some famous sales movies, like *Boiler Room* with Vin Diesel and *The Wolf of Wall Street* with Leonardo DiCaprio and *Glengarry Glen Ross* with Alec Baldwin. These are all movies that have awakened people on both sides of the sales aisle to the many interesting developments that have occurred from past to present in the art of selling. That has probably pushed innovation in the field further, because people may look for signs to see if that's being done to them so they might be a little bit harder to sell to. That has, to some degree, created stigmas on its own. Sometimes people are selling credible products, and sometimes people are selling products where there's trickery. I think all that has forced the discipline to evolve.

To be successful, salespeople in 2024 probably need to distance themselves from that stereotype than they would have had to do in 2004 or 1984 or so.

Telesales (sometimes referred to as telemarketing) was popularized in a variety of industries, including insurance in the early twentieth century, when advancements in communication technology, such as the telephone, started to become widely accessible. Insurance companies recognized the potential of reaching out to potential customers remotely rather than relying solely on in-person sales agents. This led to the emergence of telesales, where insurance agents would connect with prospects over the phone to explain various insurance policies and generate sales.

All of a sudden, salespeople could reach decision-makers directly. They could bypass their secretaries by being clever in using the telephone to get through and transform decision-makers in their thinking. That approach was commonplace and went well beyond insurance sales. It applied to every industry. It applied to people setting up legit sales organizations with legit products, and it created a lot of criticism because there were also a lot of people doing so to sell illegitimate products.

It's been an interesting journey through the evolution of technologies, which continue to advance. Today, for example, a significant portion of the lead generation process has moved online for many companies. There are now companies that sell lead research to sales organizations—leveraging database information and selling it is all they do. Before modern telecommunications technology, the process was very different.

Then it was all about relationships and who you knew, and often getting people to buy from their friends. But there are limits to that approach.

We're at a critical time for sales. Markets are tougher, and with more competition, revenue is arguably harder to come by, and you have to be better at sales than ever before if you are selling to other companies. I look at the companies that I work with who sell a wide variety of services and products. The clients who generate the most revenue have stronger sales processes and stronger methodologies for engaging those prospects when they have one-on-one meetings, which are planned and systematic and state-of-the-art. There are great products out there that just die or underperform simply because the sales process does not facilitate generating revenues, but would if they flipped to a state-of-the-art sales process.

To address the neglect of sales in the curriculum and better prepare students for careers in sales-related fields, business schools should be launching sales divisions, and they should have students take several key courses or more courses. If someone is going to become a sales specialist, or potentially a future CEO, that is one way to ensure a level of quality control.

I think business schools really need to introduce a more well-rounded way of educating students completely, which includes sales.

CEOs and Sales Experience

Understanding sales is paramount for chief executive officers because they are the ones most responsible for the generation of revenue. CEOs tend to come from one of two places. Either they invent a technology and they want to run the company selling the technology they have invented or they are the best salesperson in the company—the one who knows sales best and/or who's generated the most revenue for the company in the past, in addition to other business skills. Even within that, many technology-inventing CEOs will need to bring in sales reinforcements, or people who know sales, to hit revenue targets. This leads to a chronic problem where you often see CEOs going year after year after year with different sales leaders, always looking for the wrong things, the wrong skill set. So anyone who tries to sell a product or service through other people's contacts or by promising to leverage the contacts for sales is actually relying on a hit-or-miss sales strategy. Whereas, if you were to look at the CEOs who run the strongest organizations, you find that they're (a) very methodological, (b) very KPI-driven, and (c) understand what needs to be done to position their product in the right way to get it in front of the right people.

To make informed, factual decisions, CEOs need access to well-chosen KPIs. These help determine what needs to happen to create new clients. If you reverse engineer what that means and have that down in measurable data, you can slice and dice—that's how revenue can be created predictably. But it takes a certain type of sales leader to buy into that, as opposed to the flip side: "I'm hiring you because you know a lot of people" or "Go out and grease some palms" or what have you. Which approach is adopted depends to a large extent on the leadership and the desired approach to generating revenue in a creditable way.

Good leaders are good listeners, so I wouldn't say that a CEO must have direct experience in sales to be successful. However, certain skill sets are best learned in the trenches. If a CEO doesn't have that knowledge, it's advisable to work with someone who can transfer such skills. Being able to get coaching and/or bring in a sales leader who's going to be their right-hand person can help the CEO shape and position the product and make good decisions about driving revenue and sales.

Misunderstanding Sales

One of the reasons that sales as a broad field is misunderstood is the stigma created by universities that portray sales as the business career of last resort. Much of the tone is set there, since official disciplines such as finance, accounting, human resources, and marketing tend to be considered more high-status than sales, in part because these are the areas universities prioritize. I think the lack of sales education and the bad approaches that some people take to it have created a lot of stigma, as shown by the many jokes about salespeople being dishonest or self-interested. After all, negative comments about car salesmen run second only to lawyer jokes.

As soon as someone tries to sell you something, you start thinking, *Okay, what's their motive? Do they just want my money? Do they just want to generate commission from selling me? They're telling me that the suit looks really good, but does it really? I don't really trust what they say.*

I think this is a ripple effect from the lack of sales education since, as a byproduct, that lack creates a lot of bad salespeople, who, in turn, create a situation where people feel that sales is not a trustworthy discipline. But this can all be remedied through more sales education.

A lack of sales knowledge or expertise hurts a business. When you see companies failing and collapsing, it's basically because they're not bringing in sufficient revenue to pay the bills. So, depending on margins, everything should be fixable through increased revenue generation compared to cost cutting. If you can generate more revenues and find better ways to create more revenues, you can offset any cost problem that you have.

I'm not saying it's all about sales—you want to do both and be well-balanced. That said, I think a lot of companies feel that they have more control over costs than they have over revenue, because revenue involves, at least to some degree, looking into the future and asking, "How much money are you going to make?"

That's a pretty uncertain question, unless you have a predictable method for knowing how much and what kind of action is needed to predictably generate a specific amount of revenue. But you can reverse engineer these things with the right processes, and that's what companies often fail to devote sufficient attention to. They don't know that they have a certain amount of control over a specific set of factors to generate sales, but you're not going to operationalize that control if you're hiring slicksters or fast talkers with Rolodexes who are promising that they know people in industries, and maybe they do, but maybe they don't. You can make it predictable by knowing your customers' traits and asking, "How can I get the information into the minds of the people who can make those decisions in the right way so that they can make informed decisions? How often do I need to do that?"

The slick talkers and the data-driven analysis are two completely opposite approaches that are both called "sales."

In terms of gauging people's sales ability, it really is the "Wild West" when it comes to assessing what people know or not. It would be helpful if there were ways of standardizing certain things to know that someone who's been exposed to a certain type of thinking is at this level, and then allowing businesses to use that as a method to hire good salespeople. The other side is what's teachable and what isn't—I'll get into that later in the book. For now, let me just say that the only thing I can't teach is attitude. Because I can't really rely on anyone teaching other people sales, I'm less concerned about what they know when I meet them.

What I want to know is whether they have the right attitude. How do they learn? What occupies their minds? Are they coachable?

If I were to offer advice to business students who want to pursue a career in sales, I think the easiest way to do it is to join a company with a strong reputation for being a sales organization, with processes that involve learning from people who do it for a living and who do it very well. That probably requires a certain amount of research to find out who is good and who isn't, but in many ways, if business students want to extend their education on the job, that's probably the easiest way to do it, considering the lack of formal sales education in business schools.

More and more books are being written on sales, different programs claim to be best at teaching sales, whether it be the Dale Carnegie Sales Training course, which has been around for a long time, or more recent ones. Many sales courses profess to be state-of-the-art, and some are good, some less so. There are even people who look to teach sales on YouTube, like Grant Cardone, or use Instagram, like Jeremy Lee Miner.

I think it's really a matter of researching what brings the most to the table and where you are going to round out your gap and learn how to truly become an effective salesperson.

CHAPTER 1
Product Positioning

Product positioning is about making products that prospective customers will deem valuable, whether by solving problems or satisfying a need or want, and positioning the product to discover what people want.

This universal principle can apply to just about anything. It's important to consider that even strong products—those that solve problems expeditiously or satisfy a need or a want in an exceptional way—still need to be sellable. The difference between someone buying your product or not comes down to them understanding two things: (1) what the product does, and (2) what it can do for them in a unique way. Product positioning gives legs to the sales process and allows the sales process to bridge the gap between (1) and (2).

The Segway Personal Transporter was released back in 2001. When it was discontinued in 2020, Segway ranked alongside Sony Betamax, Google Glass, Harley Davidson Perfume, and Pepsi Crystal as one of the greatest product flops in history.

About a year before the original Segway launched, word first leaked that the inventor, Dean Kamen, had created in near-total secrecy a revolutionary transportation device, but the leak lacked specifics. Anticipation grew as those close to the project released many cryptic and exaggerated comments to the media. Apple co-founder Steve Jobs predicted it be as big as the PC, and Amazon founder, Jeff Bezos, called it "one of the most famous and anticipated product introductions of all time" before the product first went on sale to the public.

However, when the Segway was finally unveiled on live TV during the December 3, 2001 edition of *Good Morning America*, the product was a huge letdown.

Although the market for potential Segway buyers should have been huge, including anyone who can stand and has places to go, targeting everyone with such a product is not a good marketing strategy. Segway found itself wedged into the wider transportation business-to-consumer (B2C) device market as a niche product. It was missing both a clearly defined target audience and an identifiable use. Successful marketing often identifies a consumer need, then offers a product that addresses that need.

Later, Segway adjusted its approach to adopt more of a business-to-business (B2B) strategy and sought to sell more to companies and civic organizations based on the device's utility and benefits to their foot-bound associates. These included the following: the US Postal Service; police departments in Chicago, Philadelphia, and Washington, DC; fire departments; medical transportation companies; and gas companies with meter readers. Arguably, this shift in strategy came too late.

Most people don't need an alternative to walking, and there were already many low-cost alternatives, like bicycles, skateboards rollerblades, etc. Personally, I opted for an e-bike! In retrospect, weak product positioning at the outset contributed to Segway's failure. All companies need to be attentive to the importance of product positioning because it is closely linked to sales success.

Exclusive, Rare, and Valuable Products

One strategy may best apply to brand new products considered to be potentially revolutionary. A different strategy applies to products in a heavily competitive market, which use branding and/or intellectual property (IP) protection to carve out their product life and relevance in a market.

The phrase *niche crafting* refers to the process of tailoring a product, service, or content to a specific, narrow, and well-defined market segment (also known as a niche market). A niche market is a subset of a larger market that shares specific characteristics or interests or may have unique needs or preferences. Niche crafting involves identifying and understanding unique characteristics and requirements of a particular niche and then creating offerings that cater to those specific needs.

What Is a Niche?

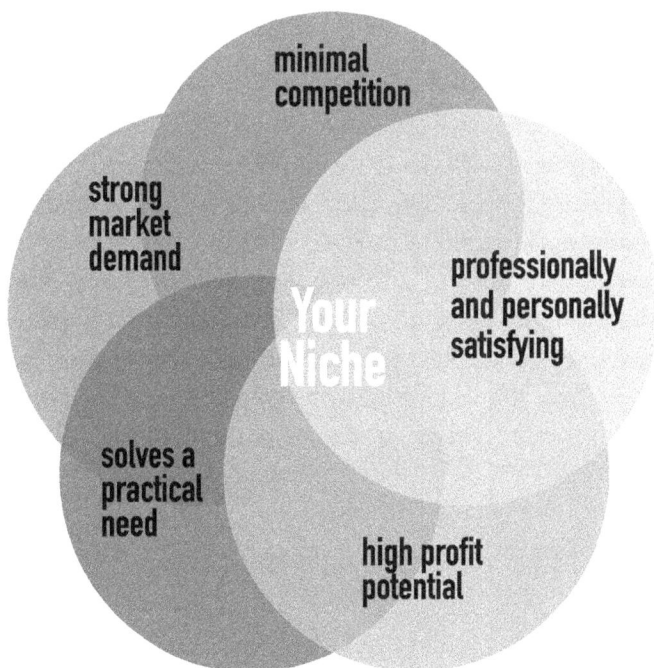

minimal competition

strong market demand

professionally and personally satisfying

Your Niche

solves a practical need

high profit potential

This could involve customizing products or services, creating specialized content, or developing marketing strategies that resonate with the target niche audience. This approach hinges on creating a level of scarcity. The psychology behind sales is that people want things that they can't have, and people value things that are rare and scarce. (In this context, "rare" means something that is not plentiful, but "scarce" means something that has limited availability because demand outstrips supply, even if it's plentiful.) Sometimes you're dealing with something like a diamond, where the corresponding scarcity means that it comes out at a certain set price. Alternatively, perhaps there is another way of positioning a particular market segment by offering a product or service to a very specific group and just doing it really well. This could involve other ways of leveraging scarcity, rarity, value, IP, or branding to accomplish that objective.

To make sure product positioning aligns with your target market needs and preferences requires A/B testing and small, nimble, isolated adjustments. Many companies perform substantial analysis when they launch a product that has multiple uses. Then there's a significant amount of strategizing about where we put our resources and what we target. Do we do it horizontally—i.e., across multiple industries at once? Or do we use a vertical strategy—one industry at a time—based on how to best approach a market, which markets to approach, and how comprehensively or narrowly to do so?

One way to do this is by having different features, or advantages, that create different benefits in slightly different ways to differentiate your products. This strategy means keeping a sharp eye on the competitive landscape: how competitors have assembled a product and how they've created either support services or extra features or integration models.

Understanding the competition and making sure that your product is a little bit different is crucial to justifying a product in the marketplace. When you're facing a decision-maker or prospective customer explaining why they should choose your product over someone else's, you need to give them valid and convincing reasons. So anyone who's positioning their product correctly is going to provide their salespeople with a pitch and package that prospective buyers will find compelling.

Many companies sell on price. Some will drop their price, which is a big part of their closing strategy and their main method for overcoming objections in price-sensitive markets. Other firms will maintain or even raise their price but add value, while others will modify the terms for purchase.

Again, these are all things that need to be thought out and adjusted in accordance with the competitive marketplace, how valuable the product is, how effectively that value can be communicated, and how exclusive and how scarce the product is.

Limiting Product Availability

One type of product positioning negates or reduces the need for the strategies outlined above to create sales. This is when a company's product or service is exclusive, rare, and valuable. A company that offers such products or services can stick to its guns, and people are still going to buy whatever it's selling. This kind of product positioning is about making sure that your product/service is take-it-or-leave-it. For instance, you can look at Apple's products, which don't go on sale, or Tesla's Cybertruck launch. People will commit to buying such products well in advance of their actual availability. They'll pay a fee as a deposit, then they're the ones who get the first call when it hits production.

So limiting or delaying production or creating a waiting list is another way of positioning your product to make sure that when it does hit the market, sales are flowing. Other examples of this strategy are pre-buying season tickets for a new sports franchise that's coming out, where teams often have a ticket drive to get, say, fifteen thousand season ticket holders. The different formulas for getting pre-buyers are all positioning strategies.

Another example of a positioning strategy comes from Costco Wholesale, where you used to need a paid membership to shop at their outlets. However, in the beginning, you could only qualify if you were a business owner or someone who worked for a company or a government or met certain other criteria. It was all about making it exclusive and rare to have a membership that created that high value. Similarly, when Google launched Gmail and you had to know someone to get a Gmail account during the beta phase, you needed a referral, and that's how they made Gmail really exclusive and rare because people would hunt around to try to find someone who had a Gmail address so they could get a referral.

When positioning products, businesses will try different things to create a sales vacuum to propel revenue. The ideal position is when sales are built into the product positioning. At other times, it's a complex sale that requires a transformative process involving salespeople who need to get customers seeing and doing things differently to make the switch to buy a product or service. The particular strategy depends on whether the product is a high-level, expensive business-to-business (B2B) item that needs to be sold to the C-suite. Advanced salespeople ask, "What is the sales strategy? Is it face-to-face meetings? Is it by phone? Is it about getting people to register online for a trial so they can experience it?"

If someone has the best product in the marketplace, a segment of the market will go after that type of product because they want only the best. Sometimes the company can position itself favorably as not necessarily the best product but the best brand.

Sometimes companies can limit availability. Other companies pursue a different strategy, such as producing and warehousing an abundance of units for a particular product but only releasing the product at the right level to meet the demand. The De Beers diamond company does something similar by restricting the amount of diamonds on the market, controlling pricing by limiting the supply.

Analyzing a product's unique set of circumstances is crucial for creating a marketing and distribution strategy that aligns with the exclusive and niche nature of the product. In some ways, that's what marketing teaches at university—and there's no shortage of people learning marketing in a university, which is one of the four disciplines of business schools. What they're not learning, though, is sales. Marketing and sales do correspond, but the sales strategy has to be aligned with the marketing.

In B2B, marketing is much less strategic and much more about lead generation. In business-to-customer (B2C) sales, marketing is the heartbeat of the positioning that propels the products and the vacuum in which people will see the product. Sales and marketing can play together, but in B2B versus B2C, they have different roles.

Every company positions its product in a certain way. Some do it better than others. When you can create a vacuum or demand, even of a viral type, it can propel your product's popularity. Take those kids' toys that take off, and all of a sudden, before the holiday season, nobody can get their hands on one, with children begging their parents to find a doll/robot/truck/plushy that's sold out.

In 1983, before Christmas, there was a Cabbage Patch Kids craze, when Cabbage Patch dolls were in such high demand that they quickly sold out in stores across the United States, leading to a frenzy among shoppers trying to get their hands on one. Now, before Christmas, there's often a toy that gets a boost in sales in similar ways because marketers deliberately try to replicate the Cabbage Patch Kids craze phenomenon.

This happens continuously. We'll take a look later in the book at *urgency* and how to create or use it. Every product out there uses a level of urgency to drive sales. This is perhaps beyond the current topic, but it's all about giving people good reasons to buy today. So every sales strategy is either one of three things: (1) an incentive to buy now, (2) a consequence for not buying now, or (3) an immediate need that causes someone to buy now because they absolutely have to have it.

I've yet to come up with any successful company that is not using at least one of these strategies. If you go to a retail store such as Macy's, and there's a Saturday sale and it's 40 percent off, the incentive is the 40 percent off, but the consequence is, if you come tomorrow, you won't get the sale price. It's always for a limited time, and that's deliberate because without limited time, there would be nothing to motivate people to take advantage of the sale price now.

Staffing resources is another important part of positioning for sales. Once you have a sales formula, you have to decide how to scale it. If it's a product that requires a salesperson, there are ways of building predictability and reverse engineering results based on knowing how many pitch opportunities by a well-trained, well-performing, gold-standard salesperson will be needed to close a deal.

Every step of that process is measurable, with different milestones to be achieved. By breaking down the steps of the process and really understanding what should happen—e.g., we are going to close at one in five, one in ten, one in fifteen, one in twenty, or one in thirty opportunities—you can look at creating thresholds along the way with the best sales process used by a salesperson and control the controllables within a margin of error.

Balancing the sales team depends on whether it's an active or passive sales approach. When Tesla was one of the only electric vehicles on the market, the product sold itself since, for anyone wanting an electric vehicle for whatever reason, whether it be a commitment to environmental causes or the cost saving associated with buying cheap electricity to power the vehicle, Tesla was the main choice. When Tesla dealerships began popping up as distribution hubs, Tesla advisors or product specialists rather than salespeople were the ones who explained the car's features, even if they are the ones technically selling the car.

On the other hand, if you take salespeople in a traditional car environment, it perhaps requires more salesmanship as they're trying to drop close, to get a commitment, often because they work on commission in a more competitive environment than, say, Tesla when it was the only electric car on the market.

Quality and Market Saturation

Quality and market saturation can affect the sales pitch or sales approach of a product. Some companies may have a product that wears out really fast, sometimes called "planned obsolescence." Planned obsolescence describes a strategy of deliberately ensuring that the current version of a given product will wear out of become out of date within a known time period, which guarantees that consumers will seek replacements in the future. Some companies are going to put a lot more money into quality so their product lasts longer. But planned obsolescence is an established way of getting people to burn through products more quickly, to always make sure that they're replacing those products on a rapid and predictable cycle. So there's also a need to upgrade—if you sell someone a lightbulb that's never going to burn out, what are you going to sell next year?

A variety of products use a subscription model, signing people up so that they buy your product every year automatically because they need it on an ongoing basis. This business model makes the first sale absolutely crucial since that unlocks current and future revenues. Other companies sell a service that someone might only buy once, then they're always having to look for new customers, so, depending upon the market, it usually takes a lot more work for new business sales than for repeat sales. Anyone positioning their product wants to create, not only a new business acquisition strategy, but as tight a repeat strategy as possible, on the assumption that customers are going to need to purchase repeatedly at a certain pace or frequency.

It's vital to balance the need to maximize growth while preserving the optics that supply is limited. As a growing business, there's usually capacity, yet a better strategy to drive sales would be to convey that a limited amount of product is available. So the conversation about the opposite of unlimited product availability is, "We have a backlog," or "We don't have product now, but pre-orders are going to take some time to be produced and delivered."

To me, it's all about giving people good reasons to buy now, and sometimes it's about "This is why we weren't talking to you yesterday; this is why there's an opportunity now, but this is why there won't be an opportunity tomorrow." It's isolating the purchasing decision at a point in time, and if that point in time passes, then the opportunity will pass as well.

Aligning Positioning with Sales Approach

Positioning *must* align with the sales approach on a product-by-product basis. Depending on how much you make your product scarce, unique, or valuable up front, especially in a market that needs it, the less salesmanship would be needed to drive sales. It's about determining what advantages you are going to exploit to drive sales. Arguably, the less time, attention, and resources you put into positioning, the more you have to put into salesmanship.

I think there is a linear trade-off in positioning between the requirements that would be needed for someone putting an awful lot into the sale and someone not doing much in this regard. For example, if you're positioning and really tightening up, everything gets you close to selling or in scoring position, such as the twenty-yard line in a football game, and then closing the sale is near: it's just a short hop to get into the end zone. When selling or playing football, are you passing the ball to the running back on your side of the fifty-yard line and asking them to run it past all the defenders all the way up the field? That is the analogy I would use when it comes to the relationship between positioning and sales.

I appreciate that my European friends might be wondering what I mean by using football as an example. To clarify, the above football analogy, which I also use several other times in this book, refers to American/Canadian football, not European football or soccer, as it is sometimes referred to in North America. As such, I apologize to my dear friends in Europe and elsewhere who make a strong claim to the word football in relation to their preferred sport.

To ensure your product is positioned well, it is important to evaluate the effectiveness of your positioning strategy. There are many ways of approaching this. In my view, setting up KPIs is a good start. You measure the extent to which a product is positioned optimally or not and where there could be efficiencies. Then shake the tree a little bit to really understand if there's room for improvement in areas that might be a little ambiguous or murky.

One way to do this is A/B testing—trying a couple of parallel strategies to see if changing one or two or three variables makes a big difference in terms of performance. The next step is to communicate your product's value proposition to potential customers.

In a B2C environment, there's television or print advertising or branding or signage—there are all sorts of B2C ways to reach large numbers of consumers. That's a whole side of sales that we'll acknowledge but won't necessarily focus on in much detail. When it comes to B2B companies who sell to other businesses, it really is a reflection of the percent cost of making the sale, compared to the total value of the sale, and to what extent a company can utilize these approaches to scale revenues while maintaining profitable margins.

That could mean engaging with prospective customers in writing, whether through emails or LinkedIn or something less formal such as texts, WhatsApp, Telegram, or Instagram. How many outreach attempts are needed to create one pitch opportunity? Would it be better to just pick up the phone to pitch prospective customers because the frequency of pitch opportunities created is higher than written outreach? How expensive is the product, and what is the cost of a sale? Is the objective to close quickly on a cheap product? If so, can you afford salespeople for setting up one-on-one engagements with prospective customers without jeopardizing margins and profitability? Or is the sale worth five, six, or seven figures, and does the key to unlocking the potential of the sale lie in a more extensive sales process?

When larger revenues generated can justify larger sales costs, many companies invest in face-to-face closing strategies. Such campaigns may begin with reps cold-calling decision-makers by phone to pitch them and set appointments to visit them in their boardrooms and later close the deal. If potential customers are more international than local, the costs of visiting them might be higher if it means getting on planes much of the time to pitch to them face-to-face However, if reps through cold-calling can build enough immediate value while giving their prospects good reasons to buy quickly without a face-to-face meeting, the cost of sales could be much lower.

Depending on whether sales can be made at predictable rates using closing by phone or face-to-face strategies, there will be significant cost differences associated with one or the other, which can greatly affect overall product profitability margins. The objective of either strategy is to turn conversations with prospective customers into closing opportunities that generate new revenues as expeditiously as possible.

Different costs and sales cycle time frames would be correlated with closing by phone compared to a sales strategy requiring a face-to-face meeting. Companies that sell expensive products internationally may have the flexibility to opt for a face-to-face closing strategy but, without testing the limits of a closing by phone strategy, may never know what might be possible, such as eliminating the face-to-face visit through more attention to product positioning, sales strategy, and better salesmanship.

Some companies have a lot more salesmanship behind their approach, but their objective is not to set up an appointment—rather, it's to deliberately engage with the decision-maker by phone, video, or otherwise with a strong proposition and sales process to close the deal. Their attitude might be more about giving people good reasons to buy today, which also prioritizes urgency and helps define the purpose of sales. Any product that is positioned in such a way makes the time frame a condition of the sale. If you can accomplish that, you're already creating that pull toward closing sooner rather than later, which is the opposite of what people would choose to do without either urgency or an immediate need.

Between those two extremes lie a lot of different choices, and I would say that the stronger the sense of salesmanship, the greater potential there is to shorten sales cycles.

I think too many companies just assume there's a relationship between the cost of their product and the length of their sales cycle. And they will accept mediocrity amongst their salespeople and sales approaches with no real understanding of what is possible or what the limits are, with respect to speeding up sales and the flow of revenues through positioning and the use of urgency.

Flexibility is key to product positioning because as customers' needs evolve, you may need to change your sales strategy or positioning approach to adapt over time to changing market conditions.

An example of changing market conditions was the COVID-19 pandemic, which almost everywhere led to restrictions in travel and regulations specifying how and when people could interact face-to-face. The product we were selling relied on delivering face-to-face meetings between buyers and sellers at five-star resorts around the world at a time when people couldn't fly or meet face-to-face. Without repositioning the product in line with these temporary restrictions, neither selling the product nor delivering the product's value to market would be possible.

We adapted by shifting all customer interactions online, something that never would have been acceptable to our clients in the absence of dire conditions. We not only survived as a business, but we also repositioned ourselves short term in a way that allowed new business sales to increase. Because the delivery of our product was transferable to setting up customer matchmaking opportunities by Zoom video conferencing, and because we already had another division that used a lot of online video conferencing technology to organize online events such as webinars for our clients, we had the technology available to allow us to make the switch. What we needed to do previously at a Four Seasons or a Ritz Carlton face-to-face, we could do over Zoom.

Those who have seen the movie *Forrest Gump* may remember the scene when the hurricane hits and Forrest is on the shrimping boat; it just so happens that his boat is the only one left floating. After that, he and Lieutenant Dan started making money in the shrimping business because they were the only boat around.

We had a similar experience, in part because our product was unique in that we were competing with other sales and marketing strategies (e.g., trade shows and conventions) and had very little direct competition. During this period, much of the value we created for our clients could be maintained even if delivery was temporarily moved online. Our clients could interact with their prospective qualified customers one-on-one using Zoom and other video-conferencing technologies.

Meanwhile, our trade show and conventions competition, where people would need to network to find qualified customers by turning a handshake into a business conversation, were canceled. A lot of our competition was out of action. All of a sudden, we were in a strong position as the only game in town, and we repositioned ourselves as a luxury brand. Although we were already an exclusive brand, we became even more so, and everyone wanted to pre-buy capacity because they felt threatened and realized that because the spots were limited, if they wanted to continue with us, they would have to make recommitments until 2024 or 2025 and beyond.

The repositioning was a huge revenue driver, and it was all true because we did have less capacity. Even if we went online, we weren't able to deliver as much product to our client base as we would have if we were at five-star resorts. There was way more demand because everyone still needed to get in front of their prospective customers. All it really took was a pitch along the lines: "We're really not in a position to take on new customers this year until we're caught up with our backlog. But if we had capacity, would you want to get involved?" In this example, product positioning following changing market conditions set up conditional closing opportunities that drove sales.

Just that little pivot of saying, "We're not overall taking on new customers this year as a general rule, but we do have a need for a company who does what you do to represent this line of business." That's a great example of how to deal with a backlog from the pandemic just by using what's happening in the world. The same applies to market forces. It's not just us; most companies are able to say, when it comes to their products nowadays: "Look, inflation is going up, and so are our costs."

Many companies basically use interest rates or inflation as justification for increasing their prices, whether or not their costs are dramatically affected.

I would cite our pivot during the pandemic as a great example of how to reposition a product in an unprecedented period. The same thing might happen during a recession. It might happen during any period when people need to readjust and find opportunities—because there are always opportunities. And where do opportunities begin and where do they end?

Some companies just milk a trend for as long as they can, and there comes a point where it's less likely that will work. When that happens, the previous strategy is replaced with another strategy that will be used to justify products being scarce or products being expensive. That's what companies do—they look at macro conditions and use them to adjust their approach to make their products either scarcer, more valuable, or more expensive.

That's the clever way to do it. You don't need to make things up—the changing market circumstances will do that for you. You just have to be observant enough to notice what's going on and use it to your advantage.

CHAPTER 2
Sales Strategy

Business to business (B2B) sales typically have a longer lifespan and involve a decision-making process that may need more than one individual signing off. Contracts are larger, touchpoints are frequent, and sales cycles are often longer.

Business to consumer (B2C) sales, on the other hand, tend to operate on shorter sales cycles since consumers are encouraged to purchase the product on the spot or shortly thereafter. B2C sales are marketed directly to consumers by mass media like television commercials, e-commerce websites, and retail sales. Although there are exceptions, retail sales are generally linked to an emotional response while corporate sales are typically well thought-out and planned.

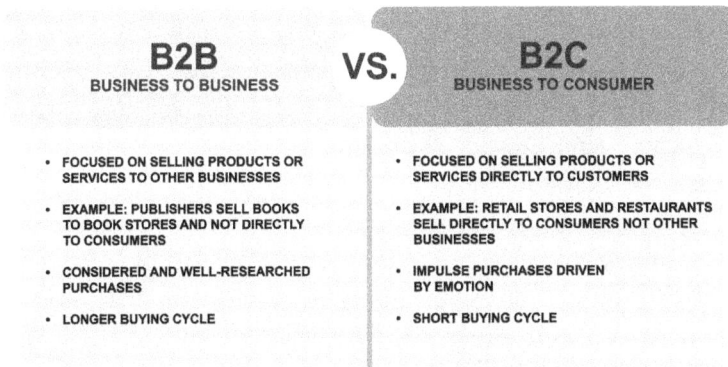

B2B BUSINESS TO BUSINESS	**VS.**	**B2C** BUSINESS TO CONSUMER
• FOCUSED ON SELLING PRODUCTS OR SERVICES TO OTHER BUSINESSES		• FOCUSED ON SELLING PRODUCTS OR SERVICES DIRECTLY TO CUSTOMERS
• EXAMPLE: PUBLISHERS SELL BOOKS TO BOOK STORES AND NOT DIRECTLY TO CONSUMERS		• EXAMPLE: RETAIL STORES AND RESTAURANTS SELL DIRECTLY TO CONSUMERS NOT OTHER BUSINESSES
• CONSIDERED AND WELL-RESEARCHED PURCHASES		• IMPULSE PURCHASES DRIVEN BY EMOTION
• LONGER BUYING CYCLE		• SHORT BUYING CYCLE

In the summer of 2023, the struggling restaurant chain Red Lobster promised its US customers an endless supply of shrimp for twenty dollars. This was a strategy they hoped would increase customer traffic and boost profits following drop-offs since the pandemic.

Although the promotion boosted traffic by a few percentage points, the number of people taking advantage of the offer far exceeded the company's projections. In an attempt to recover, Red Lobster adjusted the price to twenty-two dollars and then twenty-five dollars. Miscalculations over the popularity of the all-you-can-eat shrimp special accelerated the company's downward spiral, and ultimately, Red Lobster's filing on May 19, 2024 for Chapter 11 bankruptcy protection in the United States.

Sales strategy is important, and many companies successfully offer promotions at a loss to boost overall sales. However, this particular sales strategy seems to have put Red Lobster's entire future in jeopardy. In retrospect, it likely failed in part because the company started with too low a price point. Furthermore, they also offered as a "loss leader" a popular and pricey menu item that can serve as an entire meal.

Marketplaces and Distributors

B2B and B2C sales organizations have different ways to expose their target customers to their products. B2C can be a restaurant like Red Lobster, retail or online through their own website, or it can be a third-party marketplace, like Amazon, where customers can find a lot of different products, and outsourcing sales to a such a distributor or marketplace becomes the sales driver. The extent to which that is viable, or to which a brand lives on its own, often has to do with the level of branding—to what extent are consumers going to gravitate to that product because it's a well-recognized brand? Is this known as the best in the marketplace? Is it the Kleenex of tissues?

These are all branding elements. Then there's intellectual property (IP), which protects brands and shapes customer choices by legal mechanisms rather than salesmanship. I would say that if this were football, it's about getting the ball downfield as far as possible. If the end zone is the closing point, the extent to which a company brands a product, uses IP as a driver, or uses different distribution channels to get that ball downfield makes it a much less complicated process for putting the ball in the end zone, or getting people to say yes or no to the product.

Like Amazon, financial exchanges that trade securities are also marketplaces. Someone who wants to buy stocks can go to the stock market. Someone who wants to buy commodities can go to a commodity exchange. This doesn't really require any active sales, and financial exchanges are institutionalized and highly regulated. Amazon is similar, though it is less regulated.

There are marketplaces in B2B sales as well—well-known distributors often take responsibility for distributing a long list of products for multiple companies because of their broad reach and ability to engage decision-makers in particular vertical markets. This represents an outsourcing of the sales function by those companies listing their products for a percentage commission on products sold. Being on a distribution list could be one of several channels to distribute any particular product, or an exclusive channel.

These customer-targeting methods are used in both B2B and B2C sales and are ways of attracting customers passively. Industry magazines are tailor-made for promotional opportunities so B2B sellers can advertise directly to their potential customers. So someone who's a leader in aerospace and defense manufacturing or a medical device manufacturer can read a magazine with informative articles about aerospace and defense or medical manufacturing, while at the same time getting information about aerospace or defense or medical products through targeted ads.

These are all vehicles to either brand a product or reach to customers who may reply/engage with the ad, which also contributes to lead generation. When lead generation is the byproduct of getting information in front of customers, a more active approach may be required to follow up on leads to complete the sale, depending on the level of complexity. A big part of being out there and pursuing a more active sales strategy is a more lead-generation focused strategy, centered on putting out product information in a targeted way and getting feedback and/or creating leads through an optimized digital strategy.

It's possible to use all of these in conjunction with one another, but whether you do so or not depends on the product. The product is going to dictate the appropriate channels to use. It's often said that in B2B, the cost of sales is about 20 to 30 percent, while in B2C the cost of sales may be closer to 10 to 20 percent. Whether a company chooses to do their sales in-house or outsource or both, these are the costs. If you're entrusting your products to a marketplace that's going to create a vacuum, a place where people are just going to buy, that approach is better suited to less-complex products, typically B2C, as per the definition, as well as less complex B2B products.

If you're selling straightforward products to businesses, such as office supplies, even though you're not selling to consumers, you could certainly do that on a marketplace. It wouldn't require anything complex. The less complex the product is, the more you could probably promote it in a marketplace. You could probably use branding, and you'd probably use references and other means to get people to choose your product.

When you get into high-value business-to-business products, however, the sale is more complex. It's often a transformative sale, not a transactional one. That requires a level of trust and relationship for affirmative final decisions to be made. The products have to be creditable. They may need to pass the sniff test of multiple people. These are the nuances that tend to dictate whether a seller is going to choose a passive versus active approach. It also relates to the previous chapter, where we were talking about product positioning.

An example is the luxury brand Chanel. People favor that brand because of what it communicates—that's all positioning, if it's done in a scarce way—as Apple does with their iPhone or with other Apple products. That basically moves them all down the field and into scoring position before there has been any selling. So making the sale is about entering the end zone in a few short steps, compared to the more difficult task of running all the way up the field through the entire defense to score a touchdown, by way of analogy.

Product positioning applies to both B2B and B2C sales. In B2B sales, it's possible to position your product in a way that is in close proximity to close, or quite a ways downfield, to revisit the football analogy. So you can create a vacuum and, if you position it right, still succeed while relying on a passive strategy and without an active strategy.

Alternatively, your salespeople may simply be intermediaries who are going to facilitate the purchasing of your products by applying correspondingly consistent strategies. If you are positioning your product as a scarce brand, it would be important for any salesperson to pick that up and say, "Well, we only have so much product, and I'm not sure when we're going to be able to get it to you, and it's best you go on a waitlist." Or "We made an internal decision to sell any current availability to existing customers first, so I'm not sure if you would qualify…" Again, the positioning has to correspond to the sales strategy, which we will cover in a later chapter.

That's how the distribution strategy can impact the sales performance. If it's all distribution, and if you're just outsourcing it to an Amazon marketplace, and if that's where you do all your selling, then you're going to have to pay the fee to Amazon, and you'll be competing with other Amazon marketplace products. You probably have to make yourself stand out within that marketplace.

Other B2B lists are a different type of marketplace. Basically, you have to get on the list of a credible distributor. So, whenever someone comes up looking for a product such as yours, they can find it on the list. Their decision might come down to the star rating, product photographs and layout, product description, or reviews from other customers saying, "Yeah, we buy from this company. These are their products, they work really well, and we're happy."

There's a different dynamic with a B2B marketplace, with distributors going out and competing with one another to be seen as the be-all and end-all of having the best products in any given industry. They're jockeying for position. They're also doing branding. They're trying to get people seeking products through their marketplace.

Distribution Channels - Examples

- Field sales reps
- Corporate resellers
- Master or local distributors
- Integrators
- Value-added resellers
- Manufacturer's agents
- Brokers
- Franchises
- Telemarketers
- Inbound telesales agents
- Internet sites
- Extranets
- e-Marketplaces
- Direct mail
- OEMs
- Retail
- Kiosks
- Strategic alliances
- Agents (consultants, affiliates, etc.)

When tailoring your sales approach to end users versus other types of buyers, I would say an end-user strategy would be something like what Intel does. Intel makes an Intel chip. They advertise on TV. They want consumers to see great value in the Intel chip. And they use that to force their way into Dell or Samsung or Lenovo by saying, in effect, "Okay, consumers are going to buy more of your products if they have an Intel chip, because Intel is the premium chip that consumers want" or "consumers aren't going to buy your products unless they have the Intel chip." They have an end user strategy for making sure that the manufacturers are using their components, and they're building goodwill with consumers.

There are a number of effective marketing strategies for generating leads in the digital age. Leads are a part of the process by which visitors turn into customers. Today, lead generation is an important task for digital marketers, as many businesses need to solve the lead-generation problem if they are to grow. Lead-generation strategies include tactics to generate more traffic on a website through sales and improve the conversion rate, among many such strategies.

Often, companies optimize their website to attract customers, whether it's B2B or B2C. Being mobile-friendly can help people access your website when they're on the move. Capturing the emails of potential customers logging onto your site can be a powerful resource to get them to purchase your products. This is a fundamental lead-generation strategy and, if executed correctly, can be very effective for generating both B2B and B2C sales.

The process begins with the first stage on your website, such as providing an offer in exchange for a visitor's email address. Then you can create a targeted list of potential customers in a niche and start sending them emails. You can use email marketing to both initiate a conversation with your customers or set a date for your customers to speak with your team. That whole strategy is a very fundamental way that many companies use to generate leads that turn into sales, either through direct orders or customer engagement and salesmanship, depending on the complexity of the product.

Lead generation via social media is a fundamental part of a lot of sales in the digital era. This is how companies like Meta, Google, X (formerly Twitter), and TikTok leverage data on their customers to generate revenue, while providing free access to their platforms.

To give an example, the brand Dior is often flashing images of products on social media to get people to engage with them, and they're probably targeting higher-income customers since their products are expensive. There are all sorts of profiles meeting specific criteria that they can track, whether it's Google, Facebook, Instagram, etc. They know a lot of the customers' data profile already, including income range, so that they can target them. Then they'll put out an ad, see who clicks on it, and then try to find ways to engage customers and put a relevant product in front of them.

If it was B2C, and they were trying to sell some shoes, they might follow a progression such as the one I encountered when clicking on an ad on Facebook for Dior loafers. I was just checking out these loafers, and the first thing it said was they all were sold out after I put in my size. I thought, okay, that's interesting, and then I checked further, and they were all sold out in most other sizes also. Then a few days later, I got a prompt from Dior saying, "We have some back in stock." This online engagement got me to buy quickly to avoid my fear of them selling out again. I suspect their sales strategy was based on limiting the supply, creating an emotional reaction of regret in the mind of the consumer because they missed out, and then coming back to this consumer to close the deal—and it all seemed to be automated and done digitally.

If it were a more complicated sales strategy, such as a B2B pitch requiring a transformative experience, that whole exercise would have to be done by a salesperson. But that lead might start with someone engaging with the website, or someone wanting more information about a particular product after they've engaged with the website, with that lead then allocated to a salesperson. The salesperson would then try to create a similar dynamic as the Dior example, in getting the person to want to buy the product by building further value in accordance with a specific need or want, and creating scarcity and using urgency to give them good reasons to buy now.

There are many parallel strategies. Some you can automate, some you can't. Some have to be very active because you're driving the entire process, and some are very passive because they can be programmed, such as those based on branding, where all the work has been done because the ball is already so far downfield and in proximity to close.

Passive versus Active Sales Approaches

To actively sell a product means that you have to seek out individuals and (a) make them aware your product exists and (b) convince them that they need to buy it. Active selling is often necessary for new products that people are unaware of and new services a company offers, such as a new service or technology that has just been released. Actively selling a product is considerably more difficult than passive selling because it's more challenging to convince people who they need a product that they have never heard of. Some methods of active selling are cold calls, phone solicitation, email, LinkedIn outreach, and other forms of active prospecting.

Passive selling, on the other hand, is considerably easier and often produces a better result. Passively selling a product means that your user base is already aware of what you have to offer, and your only goal is to stand out in their mind as a preferred source to get it. It's never easier to sell a product than when people come to you wanting to buy it.

For example, the majority of Americans need insurance at some point in their lives, so by sending out helpful emails relating to the insurance industry on a regular basis, my broker reminds me that she is an excellent source for insurance, that she's available to help when needed. All she has to do is be ready to answer the phone when it rings. The trade-off here is that there is more competition in insurance than with less established products, so being top of mind or having a strong brand might be the key to unlocking sales. Otherwise, an active sales strategy, such as calling customers, might be more necessary. Passive would apply, as an example, if you set up a marketplace or became a distributor, or had other brand strategies to set you apart, or had IP protecting it so that your product was unique and couldn't be replicated.

Active sales strategies apply not only to new products but also to products that require what we call complex selling strategies, where there are multiple decision-makers and it's often a bigger spend. It requires a transformative approach to get people to buy the product. However, the better your sales approach is, the more effective you can be in transcending the complexities or the newness of your product. The better your sales process (which is further explained later in the book), the more you're able to short-circuit the difficulties of selling complex and expensive products. It all has to do with how you're going to get your products into the hands of your customers most expeditiously. That takes time and money, and sometimes the ability to have that time in a pre-revenue generating period. If it's a new product or a new service, sometimes you just don't have that time.

It's really a trade-off: if I have a product that is considered the greatest thing since sliced bread, and I have a way of describing that to people who need this product, and I can structure a sales process to get them on the phone and give them compelling reasons why they should buy this product now, I can generate a lot of revenue way more quickly through salesmanship than I would by using a passive approach.

Also, with any business that's just relying on a passive strategy, especially if it's a really valuable product, I'd be asking myself the following question: "How much money am I leaving on the table by not taking an all-fronts approach and just relying on a passive strategy, when I could be doubling or tripling or quadrupling my sales by getting my product in front of the people who would buy if they just knew it existed and was available to them—and I could identify who they are and engage with them?"

These are the decisions that everyone in business needs to make when they're creating a product—to figure out how to position the product and best sell it and extract the most revenue and find where to apply it.

Do you apply it horizontally, if it's B2B, in every industry, and really dilute the concentration of your outreach? Or do you focus on vertical markets (i.e., specific industries) that are more likely to buy because your analysis has shown which industries will be most penetrable more quickly?

Horizontal and Vertical Sales Strategies Compared

Horizontal Sales Strategy	Vertical Sales Strategy
A horizontal sales strategy is when a company targets different market sectors or industries with their products simultaneously.	A vertical sales strategy is when a company targets one sector or industry at a time with their products.
This applies when companies choose to sell to a broad target audience and diverse customer base without prioritizing one industry over another.	This applies when companies choose to put their resources towards engaging customers in one particular industry and not others.
It works best when many cross industry opportunities can be realized profitability without inefficiencies or too many duplicate costs.	It can also be justified when a product has greater value in one particular industry, or when an industry produces better results, or more revenue per sale.

Persuasion versus Resistance Selling

In the introduction, I mentioned how persuasion is what every child learns when they're two or three and they want something. "Please buy this toy for me, Mom. Come on, Mom, just buy it for me please." Whereas, as people get more sophisticated, then it becomes more a matter of making it someone else's idea. Or flipping the script so that you have positioned yourself as the prize and having something really scarce.

You might say, "We have a limited amount of product to go around, and we're very interested in partnering with companies that prioritize the environment. What could you share with me about your company's contribution to preserving the environment that would show we're allocating our resources in the right place?"

That's more about resistance and finding a point of leverage that transcends the typical relationship where the buyer has more control than the seller. In this example, the leverage comes from the company trying to appeal to customers/investors who value the environment and then challenging them to back up their appeal, compared to other companies trying to do the same thing. By positioning it that way, flipping the script as to who is in control, and reversing who is the prize, you can create leverage that can switch the power dynamic between buyers and sellers.

When navigating situations where the customer is resisting the sales pitch, it's about not being salesy but, instead, saying something like, "Look, I have a wider goal. My purpose is really to be able to make good decisions and to help our clients find solutions that are going to serve them better." That's a credible way of disassociating yourself from the perception of your motive being self-interest and avoiding some of the typical suspicions people have about salespeople.

It's important to focus on the big picture and not be shortsighted. Keep your sights on your return on investment (ROI) over the long-term, as opposed to just trying to get that quick paycheck right then and there. Whenever anyone is trying to find negotiation leverage with prospective customers, through either product positioning, scarcity of availability, or applying resistance, the way facts and unique circumstances are presented can determine whether the strategy accomplishes its objectives or not. It all has to be done with sensitivity, conviction, and good reasons that preserve your objectivity and credibility.

For instance, Rolex has stores all over the world. It is extremely hard to buy a Rolex right now in a store, post-pandemic especially, presuming that their production of watches slowed during that time because labor supply was lessened. All they say is, "Okay, we'll put you on a waiting list, and we will call you when one is available." They have always had waiting lists for their most exclusive watches, but now it seems to be across the board with all of their watches. If you've bought Rolexes before and you're in their database, they'll probably come to you first. If they come to you because you're on a waiting list, they will say, "Okay, you have twenty-four hours to show up with money to get your Rolex or we're going to the next person." They have limited the supply of their product to such an extent that they dictate the terms of who gets it. It's very, very strict, and people just have to accept that.

Creating Pitch Opportunities That Close Predictably

A key element in sales is creating pitch opportunities for sales teams to close predictably. This ties into what we're going to deal with in Chapter 5 when it comes to KPIs. Whenever you're deciding how to describe your product, certain fundamental things need to be in a pitch. Knowing what those elements are—which we'll get into later—and positioning them or sequencing them in the right way to make the message absorbable is key. Seeding that message with emotional triggers that are going to evoke desire in customers, and doing that at the right level of frequency—because sales is a numbers game too—will create patterns that are observable and can be measured. These patterns can be utilized to refine the product description while anticipating results predictably.

This is about creating a system from scratch that—going back to aligning product positioning with the sales approach— wherever you are on that continuum or wherever the ball is down the field, combines a series of features and steps and descriptors and components that is the sales pitch in itself.

Then the key is to A/B-test it in different ways to look for patterns to see (a) when it is working at its best compared to other ways of sequencing and other combinations, and (b) when we do this repeatedly, and have different people apply it, and what a comparison of the results show.

We isolate and control all the variables in a way that reveals patterns and makes decision-making around sales strategy much clearer. When we allow different sales reps to pitch decision-makers a product, and we train them a certain way, and best practices are applied correctly, patterns will be revealed that show, for example, that every five to ten pitch opportunities will predictably lead to a sale. If those closing ratios, once established, are not maintained, it can be logically deduced that different reps are doing something wrong. Using KPIs in this way to identify what reps are doing wrong and suggesting thoughtful solutions can become the key to maintaining predictable sales outcomes and ironing out inconsistencies in individual and collective sales performances.

Once you establish those baselines, you can use performance data to effectively set gold-standard selling processes, define the characteristics that the salespeople you hire need, and give them a blueprint of how they need to perform to get the income they want through commissions, while also forecasting future revenue.

When it comes to the potential for technology, especially AI, to create a better, testable pitch than can be adapted by a human, I think it only goes so far. It's one of the reasons why I believe sales will never be replaced by AI, especially if it's the complex type of sales requiring processes that we'll explore more deeply later in this book. The most savvy salespeople will learn AI and use it to their advantage and save time, much like how the calculator replaced the need for many people to rely on manual arithmetic. Many other things are going to be automated. A lot of simpler sales strategies will be automated in the future, and they're not going to require salespeople, but there will always be a complexity of sales that can never be replaced by technology.

We're looking here at how active and passive strategies in both areas of sales dictate the amount of work that's prepackaged and pre-done versus work that needs to be done each and every time on the spot. Many decisions need to be made along the way to decide how far downfield you want to put your product and then build a strategy around closing and the creation of revenue. That's going to dictate the passive-versus-active ratio in your sales strategy and how often each comes into play (although, with some complex products, a passive strategy may not add much).

However, for some products, it's potentially irresponsible to rely solely on passive sales and not to add an active strategy and have both contributing to revenue generation, because each strategy will accomplish different things.

This brings us to a crucial issue in this book: in addition to the contrasting strategies of B2C and digital sales etc., complex B2B products that are expensive, and which require top executives to sign off on budgets, demand a higher level of salesmanship. This comes into play when a product can only win the support of a top executive through quality salesmanship of quality products. The level of sales achieved for such complex products will be heavily influenced by the sales strategy and the salespeople making the pitch. In such circumstances, there is plenty of extra revenue to be generated for companies if they utilize state-of-the-art selling processes.

Much of what follows in the book will explore what's necessary when a company decides that it needs to build a sales team to sell to other companies, how to develop that sales team, and how to measure the performance of that sales team through KPIs. After that, the next stage is to use the work of that sales team to find patterns to use to adjust your future positioning and refine how you're going to deal with changing market circumstances. Once you have a set plan that's optimized, we'll discuss how you can accelerate it through hard work and how that compares to people just giving extra attention to executing the sales process at the highest level of proficiency.

Both approaches can contribute to success. We will also look at other small elements that make a difference in how much companies are able to capitalize on revenue generation opportunities and how to optimize that more and more through different processes, technologies, and closing approaches.

CHAPTER 3

Choosing a Sustainable Sales Team

Risks versus Rewards of Hiring Salespeople with Contacts

When hiring a sales team, many firms go with slicksters or Rolodex keepers, which is how I more or less jokingly label these types of salespeople, because hiring them tends to be one of the most common ways that people building a sales team try to bolster their capacity to penetrate any target market. This is particularly true in B2B sales, when they believe that in a particular vertical sector or with certain C-level prospects—if that's how they're approaching it—they need connections to create sales pitch opportunities. The number of pitch opportunities created represents the top of the funnel and erodes, because it is a numbers game, so there are different ways of approaching it.

The reason I call them slicksters or Rolodex keepers is because these are typically people who talk a big game and claim to know everyone. They've usually been in sales or an industry for a while, and they'll sell people in a job interview on their ability to create magic in helping them penetrate the market through their natural skills, contacts, and/or prowess at opening doors. The challenge is that it's very risky to hire that way.

For one thing, it's often hard to validate such claims. For another, if someone is successful using that approach, it's hard to teach or replicate. Often, it's like a nonrenewable resource—

eventually, it runs out. That approach can also create dependence on that particular individual or that particular approach, which can prevent a company from selling sustainably and scaling over the long term.

I'm not saying you can't utilize a sniper approach on occasion, where you might bring in someone who can open a lot of avenues to the C-suite. That is definitely a bona fide way of trying to create revenue in a targeted way. But if that is the be-all and end-all of your sales approach, if you are hiring a VP of sales in hopes of hiring a team of people who already have that industry experience to open doors, that's not the most sustainable approach.

Finding the right people and developing them into the role is a longer-term play. It is analogous to sports teams that build up through the draft and player development, as opposed to signing a bunch of free agents to try to put together a winning team to go after the championship right away. In major league baseball, for example, one approach is to draft people who are great athletes with the right attitude, then try to develop them into superstars. That tends to be the long-term play. It's a play that can be repeated over and over because it's a process. Given the right methodology and the right adjustments, it can be fairly predictable.

The flip side of that, of course, is short-term gain, which carries with it the danger of bringing in the wrong person who isn't going to succeed. At one point earlier in my career, I noticed that the lifespan of a VP of sales in a B2B sales organization tended to be very, very short—probably one of the shortest tenures of any executive class in many companies. This was because so many companies, for a long time, were just bringing in the wrong people based on promises of short-term results. And because a lot of companies have longer sales cycles, it might take them eight or ten months to realize that a particular individual is never going to sell anything. The person might be able to name a host of people, but can they engage with them? Will they fail because they are terrible at opening or terrible at closing or other aspects of a sound and predictable sales process?

The risks with that kind of approach are quite high. Whereas if you go to the flip side and find a methodology based on the characteristics of your best salespeople—just like a major league baseball team might have a profile for their best potential future players based on athleticism—you can take that and exploit it. You can nurture it and create a replicable model that's data-driven, measurable, and logical, creating longevity and the capacity to renew that process over and over instead of trying to find that free agent, that person with all the contacts in the world, which is probably more hit-and-miss than many people might think.

Here's a famous Thomas Edison quote: "Genius is one percent inspiration and ninety-nine percent perspiration." Mark Cuban said, "Talent without effort is wasted talent. And while effort is one thing you can control in life, applying that effort intelligently is next on the list." Cristiano Ronaldo, when describing the hard work that goes into his training, said: "Talent without work is nothing."

In my experience, the hardest thing to teach anyone in sales is attitude. That's because usually people who change their attitude over time do it on the basis of an epiphany, a humbling experience, or something that causes them to see things and do things differently at a worldly level. Given that it is so rare and hard to teach, that would be the trait I would look for before anything else when selecting a salesperson.

When I talk about attitude, I'm usually talking about a person's level of positivity or negativity. These are words that are difficult to measure precisely because there are different interpretations. But hiring someone with a positive attitude is the most important thing for any sales culture, because salespeople typically hear "No" way more than "Yes."

Sales is a game of failures, and with the wrong attitude, people can lose faith quite quickly and start to blame external factors for their lack of success. What salespeople need to do is to look humbly in the mirror and truthfully recognize what they do well, what they don't do well, and address their weaknesses, meticulously turning them into strengths.

Learning Styles and Characteristics of Top Salespeople

Another way to determine the traits of a good salesperson is to categorize their learning style. There are different ways of understanding how people learn. Everyone has a certain knowledge and skill set, and if you're hiring someone for a technical position, there's only a specific cohort of people who can do that job. My preference would still be to find someone with some fundamental skills with the right attitude, because someone with the right attitude likely isn't going to destroy your culture, likely isn't going to cause problems within your organization, and likely isn't going to cause people to be noncompliant or fight against the rules that are in place.

Testing learning styles can be done in many ways. We'll get into the measurement description later in the book. Different systems measure different attributes of people's personality, whether it's psychometric or other forms of testing designed to break down people's personality and learning styles and give employers a profile to put them into a high-probability box or not. I usually try to keep it simple so I can compare a few attributes. Most of the time, I want to understand the candidate's personality type.

Many salespeople are *activist personality types*, for example. Activists tend to be, "Go, go, go!" They tend to just want to do things. They might not read the instruction manual—when they get that piece of equipment, they're probably just going to be inclined to put it together intuitively.

If I'm managing an activist, I'm probably going to realize that to get them to do it my way, I may need to repeat myself dozens of times. That's just the way they learn. But if you don't understand that they're an activist, you might miss the bulk of their potential. Understanding that's how someone learns and how their behavior corresponds to that is important from a management perspective.

The same thing applies to someone I would define as a *reflector*, which is another type of learning style. If I identify a reflector through whatever testing we do, I'm not going to repeat myself. I'd probably pull them aside at the end of the day and say, "Have you ever thought about doing it this way?" Often, the next day, after reflecting, they will try to implement it.

Theorist is another learning style. A theorist may just need to know the reasons we apply a particular process when selling a product, so taking the time to give them an in-depth explanation might be the best thing you could do. Other people are pragmatic—they just want to know what's in it for them every step of the way, especially when closing their client requires a takeaway to get it done.

Many people have combined learning styles, and so understanding how people work—there are good performers within all those learning styles—and getting the most out of them have to do with interacting with and adapting to them.

There are other ways of looking at learners as well.

For a long time, I went through a lot of failures in trying to figure out some of this methodology. I was hiring way too many slicksters and people overpromising things, people who sounded good—but with the wrong attitude. These days, I use a test that is very good for understanding people's tendency to remain positive in the face of adversity or going negative and blaming external factors for their lack of success in any given moment.

There's also a grit test that measures people's likelihood of finishing things they start. Applying testing to help measure attitude reduces dependency and the time required to administer psychological interviews, and helps interviewers to use this process to hire better future salespeople.

Usually, I would want someone who has high grit and high positivity. Someone with negative tendencies and high grit is a risk to me because while they might never give up, they continue to fail and always blame external factors. Comparing, running people through the system, observing the characteristics of top performers, and maintaining data on those characteristics can create a profile over time of the ideal choice of candidate when selecting future top performers.

Tailoring training programs to support many different learning styles is the safest way to accommodate the diversity that is inevitable in a sales team. That's why role-playing, case studies, and exercises are often where the most advanced trainers bring subject matter to fruition in the learning experience.

There are also Gagne's nine events, which can enhance learning and recall in diverse learners by applying a set of fundamental steps to every learning experience.

Many planning elements can impact the creation of a sales team, and all need to be executed properly. A variety of process training and retraining should be given to all salespeople to ensure the process they are utilizing to communicate their value proposition to their potential customers, and to create closing opportunities, is being applied in a state-of-the-art way. When possible, this can involve tape training, which is when a senior person in sales reviews the tape of someone newer in sales to pass on best practices. If you are reviewing an employee's sales process with a tape and it goes off course, you need to understand why that happened, how they can stay on track next time. Being in a position to teach this is paramount.

That's a lot of factors to consider, not only in hiring, but also the next step in continuously training salespeople. It's all about controlling the controllables and knowing that if you have the right raw piece of clay, you can turn it into a beautiful piece of art by nurturing it in the right way.

Learning is a big part of that, and it's predictable—when the processes that are applied to a good candidate are pure, the outcomes tend to be pure and predictable as well. It all comes back to the theme that we'll continue to talk about, which is the "predictability of sales."

Attitude versus Experience and Measurable Capabilities

Attitude allows for better cultural fits. My target profile is positive people who typically succeed at what they set out to do. When it comes to overall success, it's more important to have a salesperson with an awesome attitude and personality than it is to have someone with a long list of certificates and a bunch of Rolodex contacts, who may or may not help your business. If you make the wrong choice, you can tip a sales force and a sales culture in the wrong way very quickly and create a mutiny or people who don't believe in the product, don't believe in the leadership, don't believe it's possible, and who will blame the company for their failure.

So grit, resilience, the potential to adapt to new approaches, the humility to fail, the ability to reinvent themselves and recover—these are all characteristics that feed into the culture you want. If you can create a culture of commitment to such principles, it can sustain different attitudes.

Building a strong culture around the right principles allows you to bring in different types of people and shape them with the program, whereas if you never fix the culture, you're always way more vulnerable to one new or established person coming in and turning your salesforce upside-down when the going gets tough.

When you have a group of negative people, my position is that if it's going to limit you, you may have to start afresh at a certain point. In more than one place, I've had to really look at the people—either they're helping or hurting what I'm trying to do. I've had people who have had epiphanies along the way, who have realized that approaching things positively makes everyone win, and they've changed. But I've also had to deal with people who we couldn't fire at will due to local employment laws.

In one case, such a person was a multimillion-dollar performer, but in this particular jurisdiction, it was hard to fire someone who had been in a company for that long. However, this individual made a grave error, which gave me the right to let him go. This was helpful mostly because his presence was unsustainable when it came to onboarding future top sales performers into the company.

So here I was, taking millions of dollars out of our revenue stream by removing this person, and the next year, our sales actually increased significantly. Part of that had to do with the fact that this very charismatic guy would put his arm around every new person coming into the company to show them the ropes—he would smoke cigarettes with them outside or talk to them at the water cooler and tell them paranoid stories about what they needed to look out for, and why the company wasn't as cool as they thought it was, and that shaping people at the onboarding stage was costing us so much money.

My firing him paid for itself many times over. It was a tough call to make, but it had to be done.

That particular change allowed me to instill a new culture through positive managers. Sometimes the bold move is necessary for getting rid of the monkey on the back of an organization that always seems to be taking two steps forward, one step back or, worse, because of the attitude of experienced people who just aren't going to allow it to thrive.

In balancing attitude and experience when building a high-performing sales team, the optimal approach depends on the technical nature of the work and the teachability of the job. The best formula is to have both, but experience can be a negative as well if someone needs to unlearn what they learned elsewhere to comply with your processes. There are times when, instead of taking someone with a lot of experience in the more needy, persuasive side of sales, or the customer service side of sales, and plucking them into a resistant sales position, you might be way better off hiring people right out of university with the right attitude. After all, you don't want to spend months getting people to try to unlearn things who are just never going to be successful in your particular environment.

I believe a hundred percent that someone with less experience who has a positive attitude can outperform a more experienced but negative person. Not every time, but I would put my money on positive people who typically succeed in the things that they set out to do, given the fact that sales usually involves teaching people a whole new skill set. If someone's done something identical, and their experience is in line with it, and there's not a lot of change required as far as how they approach the sales process, and they have a great attitude, they're probably going to outperform because they're going to get to it way more quickly. But that's a tough combination to get. I want to find people like that. I don't always know where to look.

Take the example of Satya Nadella, who became the CEO of Microsoft in 2014. He had both a desire and an opportunity to change the culture of Microsoft when he took over. It was a very similar process—there was a lot of resistance to new ideas and declining innovation. Certain people, who were stuck in the past and wouldn't allow new ways, were stifling innovation. My understanding is that Nadella basically came in and said,

"This is the change I'm requiring of you. Either you get on with it or not. If you don't, you're going to have to go."

Some people got on with it. Some people didn't. When he took over the company in 2014, the market capitalization was $316 billion. By 2020, following this cultural change, the market capitalization of Microsoft was $1.2 trillion. So it's a tried-and-true approach that doesn't only apply to sales teams but also to any mature organization that is looking to reinvent itself and find a new gear in performance.

You don't have to be loud and boisterous to generate revenue. A lot of quiet people are great salespeople because they're very thoughtful. These are people who other people trust. They tend to use words carefully. They may be highly teachable and/or strong implementers and can be very good at using processes that have a high degree of precision in allowing them to almost disarm someone and close more sales.

I can think of two people I worked with who didn't even need a process. They were just so good that they got commitments from customers that other salespeople couldn't. They were just very, very convincing. The problem was, they had trouble building a team because it was very difficult to teach people what they were doing. Then, all of a sudden, they became managers, but not good ones. They had a high staff turnover because what they did was not replicable, and their inability to find people who would sell like them made their success unsustainable. Some individuals are just great salespeople and are going to do it a different way. As long as that doesn't threaten your core sales culture with how other people sell or cause people to figure it out themselves, such individuals can usually be managed in a manner that doesn't disrupt the company.

Measuring Attitude and Grit

As I mentioned earlier in the chapter, to effectively measure a candidate's attitude and grit during the hiring process, I would look at personality tests, learning style tests, grit tests, and tests that measured people's propensity to remain positive in the face of adversity. I would combine that with some calibrated interviews, which included questions that reveal people with the wrong mindset. For example, I would ask someone, "What bothers you?" I'm not saying it works every time, but somebody might go off on a victim's rant, blaming everyone for their terrible life and so on, and that's going to show something that might not have been exposed if I hadn't asked that question.

There are questions that you definitely want to ask that are going to block hires who might pose threats to the company. Again, there's testing that companies can do: the interview process, the phone screen process, the first interview process, the secondary process, etc. Maybe there's a third interview. Maybe there's a panel. These should all be designed to accomplish different things. You want to ask why being successful in the job is important to them, so you can understand that "Why" and use it to motivate them in different ways. Usually, I try to understand someone's predictability of future performance or their development ceiling, in choosing a high-performance team through an interview process.

Some sales organizations burn and churn, with no idea what kind of person they're hiring. They throw people into the deep end and end up firing a lot of people, and only the strongest survive—which, at best, is inefficient and, at worst, very costly.

I'm not saying that's how our company functioned in the beginning, but there were inefficiencies in that we really didn't know exactly how to hire or identify which individuals had a high probability of succeeding in our environment and which didn't.

Now that we go through all these hiring processes, it's very rare that we bring someone in who doesn't do well. Then it's about keeping things moving in a positive direction. Jack Welch said in his book *Winning* that you always want to replace the bottom 10 percent of any sales team, because that's how you can bring fresh people in—you get rid of the lowest performers, and you up the bar.

Larry Ellison from Oracle allegedly advocated firing the lowest-performing salesperson at the end of every month, because raising the stakes can also boost performance amongst those who survive. Whether this approach is sustainable or not is hard to say, but some would consider such practices to be brutal forms of management that could impact the corporate culture and incur other costs as a side effect. You need to be getting good ROI, and if done tightly, that process can yield great results. If someone is not being attentive to these objectives, it's a missed opportunity. Companies might as well burn money in the fireplace if they're not trying to rigorously identify the most important attributes of an ideal salesperson.

I handle the goal of refreshing the sales team, which touches on the KPI tracker that will come up in Chapter 5, by measuring performance. Measuring performance through that onboarding period is the key to knowing if someone is predictively going to be closing deals or not. It's not about telling people, "You suck" or "We're firing you." It's about saying, "This is what isn't working, and let's come up with a plan for turning an identified weakness into a strength. This is what you need to do. This is what we're going to do, and let's come back and talk in two weeks or a month, and see what's been accomplished, and we're going to measure it in the meantime."

If it still isn't being addressed, at a certain point, you need to make a decision. People in sales usually reap the benefits of a commission structure, and continuing with them doesn't make sense for the employer or the employee if they're not generating results.

People need to pull their weight. If someone doesn't teach them that, they're possibly going to fail to do that, threatening their career and maybe not getting anywhere, At the end of the day people must be held accountable. It's not about making snap decisions or irresponsible decisions or pulling someone out of the sales team and saying, "You're fired" because of your ego if they crossed you in some way. That's never the case. It's about saying, "This is what we agreed to in the plan based on the trajectory of performance. You agreed to that plan. You signed up for that plan. You haven't achieved that plan. You need to find a way to remedy that, or this isn't going to work."

The following are key steps for building a culture of grit and resilience at a company:

- ❖ Set clear, achievable goals.
- ❖ Provide support.
- ❖ Encourage risk-taking and trying new things.
- ❖ Recognize/reward success.
- ❖ Foster a positive team culture.

When it comes to building successful high-performance sales teams, every office that I've been responsible for has featured a slightly different combination of people in place, as well as different challenges. It was all about being able to come up with a customized plan each and every time I was given the responsibility of building this type of sales team.

To use coaching to develop your sales team and help them reach their full potential, identifying strengths and weaknesses is the first step. This can be done through performance evaluations, sales metrics, and feedback from peers and prospective customers or existing customers. Once strengths and weaknesses have been identified, sales leaders should set clear goals and expectations for the team, and these goals should be specific, measurable, achievable, relevant, and time-bound (SMART goals), which is often considered the best practice.

Then provide training and development opportunities. Leaders should provide their team with the training that they need to succeed—this could be sales training or product and professional development programs. I'm often rotating between process training, sometimes tape training, because we can listen to the live calls, motivational training, and planning and/or strategy meetings.

The key is to understand what will make the biggest difference day to day in the salesperson's activity and how to use time effectively to propel their development.

The biggest misconception about what it takes to build a successful sales team is the idea that salespeople are born and not made. I think it is too often promoted that it's natural talent, that some people have the gift or some people are just born selling, and that personality traits such as confidence are not skills that people develop. That really has its pivot point in fixed-mindset thinking versus growth-mindset thinking.

A fixed mindset is all about talent, natural talent, whereas in a growth mindset, people believe that their most basic abilities can be developed through dedication and hard work. A lot has been written about growth versus fixed mindsets in recent years, and that definitely applies to sales. The only thing that can't be taught in sales is attitude, which is why that's the golden nugget I search for, first and foremost, because most other things can be brought out in people through growth.

Another obstacle is the belief that sales is all about hitting quotas. That is not what this is about. It's about successful sales teams needing to foster and build long-term relationships with customers, provide excellent service, and adapt to changing market conditions—and that takes an all-fronts approach. These all feed into hitting high sales numbers.

I think setting targets is a more positive way of measuring performance. It also creates a way to incentivize people. Having targets is the way many sales organizations become profitable, the more people achieve, the more you can pay them.

Recently, I was team building with one of my offices, and people were joking with me about what we used to do back when I was learning how to sell. I made a joke about how there weren't even calculators in my day, just an abacus. Levity aside, I told them that when it came to who we targeted for employment and how we conducted lead research, it was simplistic and definitely "old-school". We had ways of getting a magazine to send us lists of advertisers, and we would just basically call anyone who advertised in the magazine. There was way less technology—just the phone and trying to get them to sell.

Now, everyone is using LinkedIn and databases. I remember when search engines were coming into play, nobody knew whether to use Ask Jeeves, Lycos, or Google. Obviously, Google prevailed. There were all sorts of crazy search engines out there, and nobody really knew which was best. Now, everything has been automated to the point that without a CRM, without ways of being able to use technology, companies will be left behind.

It's a whole different world. The people who didn't adapt fell by the wayside.

CHAPTER 4
Maximizing Sales Team Development

Onboarding Plan

An onboarding plan is important for developing a sustainable, high-performance sales team. When bringing in a team, you need to find the right balance between classroom training for sales teams and one-on-one training, if you're not hiring in a group. Other methods can also be used to teach new employees the fundamentals they need to succeed at the job. A typical plan might evolve after a salesperson is given a certain amount of orientation about the company, the product, and the fundamentals of sales training. There should be some theory underlying the methodology and several modules developed for new salespeople to read or learn in a classroom. That's often going to become a prospecting plan that can help new employees hit the ground running.

Airbnb focuses on creating a positive and immersive onboarding experience for new employees. They have a dedicated onboarding team that guides new hires through an orientation program, which includes training sessions, team-building activities, and exposure to the company's culture and values. Airbnb also provides ongoing learning and development opportunities through their internal learning platform.

A common prospecting plan deals with finding high-probability leads—how to identify companies that business analysis shows are likely to buy your product, as opposed to this process being entirely a numbers game, like prospecting by using the phone book. How can you discern characteristics that customers have in common that make it easier to profile and narrow down lucrative prospects in big markets? How do you time-manage the process of locating high-probability targets and diversify so your reps are not just approaching the same potential customers with the same idea, neglecting other likely prospects? Teaching people how to do that type of research is crucial.

Then you begin teaching your people how to reach a prospect. Is that a matter of approaching people through emails, through LinkedIn, calling people? The third phase might be about pitching the product. Setting calls and learning how to set calls through emails and/or phone calls might be different than prospecting or pitching. When a person is learning how to pitch, that's a whole different exercise as well.

The old-school way would be to push someone into the deep end of the swimming pool, which could mean getting them to pitch all by themselves, perhaps after providing them with a sales pitch put together by other salespeople or managers. This pitch, if delivered at a high level of performance by any salesperson—meaning an Academy Award–winning performance sounding perfectly spontaneous—could let even new reps find sales success, once they have the desire, ingenuity, and capability. At the very least, such a process would give new reps the chance to practice so they could gain experience, allowing them to make adjustments and modifications themselves under the guidance of management.

Other companies choose to develop new sales talent through an apprenticeship model, where they'll match people up with a sales leader and have that sales leader pitch people opportunities that they've set up. Then the onboarding plan would be more about learning how to sell by listening to and observing the sales leaders. That could apply to B2B sales that are set up that way. It could also apply to someone who is learning in a retail environment, where they watch someone else pitch a prospect, then later apply to other customers what they've learned through observation.

This type of sales learning would be through the lens of other people, observing their approach, with the new salesperson slow-playing their own involvement.

Another phase in this type of development is getting the rep involved in some sales calls led by a more experienced sales leader. This type of participation can be compared to the training wheels used by my five-year-old nephew. After enough practice, the training wheels can come off, and just like my nephew learning to ride a two-wheeler bicycle, salespeople can be onboarded in similar ways.

Nevertheless, some salespeople would be frustrated by having to learn with training wheels, so for those more inclined to say, "Put me in the game, coach," a better onboarding plan might be to use a trial-and-error approach, not holding them back and just allowing them to pitch from the beginning.

Finding an optimal balance between these three options— deep end, apprenticeship, observation—is important. This is why it's crucial to have an onboarding plan that sets out objectives people are supposed to reach after a certain number of days on the job, specifies where people need to be, and defines what types of coaching, training, learning and reviews need to be done throughout that critical onboarding period.

Measuring that while hand-holding people through onboarding is important—sometimes it's valuable to have an end-of-day debrief or a weekly lunch just to come together and express frustrations and vulnerabilities.

If someone feels that they're in over their head, you don't want to be turning people over, for obvious reasons. You don't want people to be freaking out or pressing the panic button if they discover that sales is harder than anticipated. It is helpful for experienced salespeople who have overcome such challenges to provide reassurance to new sales reps. There are ways of optimizing the onboarding process, taking into consideration the uniqueness of any business.

If you don't do the onboarding process well, you can lose high-potential salespeople because of inefficiencies and not controlling the controllables. You need to both select the right people and execute a flawless onboarding plan. There should be transparency about how hard the job may be. The right people will tend to gravitate to the challenge, especially when the rewards associated with figuring out the job are massive and beneficial. You want people to know what to expect, the level of support they have, what they're responsible for, and what others will help them with.

To onboard new sales team members effectively, I recommend a few fundamental steps:

- ❖ Effective training or a training school
- ❖ An effective transition into the sales environment; work with their team
- ❖ A twenty, forty, and eighty-day plan that is going to map out where people are and what they need to be accomplishing every day, which lets us know whether someone's ahead or behind on that pace, so we can make decisions to intervene or assist in a nimble and supportive way

To ensure that your sales team receives ongoing training and development opportunities the best practice is a standardized procedure that outlines what types of training people should be getting at what point in their development. That needs to be built over time by those who went before, through knowledge and an acquired understanding of what the best practices are.

Training: Process, Tape, Motivation, and Planning

While there's more than one way to sell, standardizing is very important in running an effective sales team. You don't want half your team doing sales one way, and half doing it another way (unless you are in testing mode).

Once clear, everyone needs to buy into the plan and commit to putting in the work to learn the plan. There are many reasons why it is essential for people to buy in and stick to the same playbook moving forward until, collectively, adjustments can be agreed on and implemented to improve the sales process.

When introducing a new sales process or technique, it's important to train your team properly. Weekly or monthly meetings/conference calls can be set up to discuss an innovation that is working in one part of the company, e.g., if I have a sales leader who is training on not giving away a certain element of the product too soon to create conditional closing opportunities, I want regular opportunities to share such best practices.

Quotas—or targets—and commissions are not the only tools for motivating sales teams to achieve goals. Different people are motivated by different things. Some people are motivated by financial success. Others are motivated by professional success in the form of promotion. Other people are motivated by personal development, while others want recognition before other achievements. Still others are motivated by travel and exciting experiences.

The way I see it, it's important to understand what motivates your people by utilizing the right kind of testing and interviewing. Anything under the sun can be considered if it motivates and makes sense and can be justified because it creates a sufficient uptick in sales performance, even if specific to one person.

The flip side of that is goal setting, because sometimes I can set someone a nonmonetary incentive, and depending upon how their mind is charged, the result may or may not be positive. We will explore this further later in this chapter, but I once set an incentive for an up-and-coming manager: to spend a month at our London office if she only achieved another sale. We had set the bar low because we wanted her to hit the target. Unfortunately, she was paralyzed by the challenge, because she wanted it so badly. All of a sudden, her sales stopped. Because goal setting is tricky, depending upon whether a person's mind is positively or negatively charged about their goals, the process might be helpful or hurtful. It's either going to bridge a gap between where they are and where they want to be, or it will widen the gap. This is because when people set goals, they sometimes psychologically process the objective through a negative filter and become fixated on not having achieved the goal rather than making progress toward the goal.

If goal setting is done with people who focus on the absence of the desired achievement, it may backfire. The managers who are using goal setting to drive sales need to be aware of what those risks are and how to change the goals in a way that's going to enable people to achieve. That entails teaching people that what is important is believing that they can accomplish the goal, as opposed to obsessing over the fact that they haven't achieved it yet.

Benchmarking and Accountability

Through benchmarking and being able to understand the different development trajectories people take, you can get a clear picture of what works at your company and what doesn't. Different salespeople have different roles. Some salespeople may sell only for themselves. Others may be really good at generating consistent sales every year but also might be great teachers of the job, or they might be great managers that people want to work for. Others are go-getters and are going to sell products at a higher pace. Some are well-rounded and good at everything. A number of different trajectories lead to success, and different people in a good sales team will use various types of sales strategies.

To encourage collaboration and teamwork among your sales team members, you should employ proven methods for building healthy teams. This requires ensuring that your salespeople realize that someone else's gain is not their loss, while engaging in healthy competition for motivational and benchmarking purposes. In markets where the prospect pool has been accurately estimated, the pie is big enough for everyone. The accomplishments of others simply serve to show what's possible.

There are ways of having people play different roles on the team, and hiring with that attitude in mind is generally going to have people see the glass half full as opposed to half empty. I'm probably not going to hire people who believe that someone else's success is their loss because I don't want them bringing the baggage that an unhealthy attitude can create. But I also like when they are competitive and fight to be better, using benchmarking to compare themselves to other reps to explore what's possible.

Then there's management's responsibility. One leader I came across pitted his sales directors in different offices against one another, so just about every time one office made a successful transaction or a deal, he would rub it in the faces of the others. Showing what was possible was the main motivation, but the byproduct was that all the leaders and sales directors hated one another and were reluctant to come together as a team.

My view is, why would any leader want that? What is really needed is a way to build strong teams, have everyone believe that the teams are greater than the sum of their parts, and nurture that through a variety of systems.

It's important to be supportive and not judgmental and let people sound off about what isn't working. It's not about being negative or blaming external factors, but an attitude shift is needed if someone tells me that nobody's answering the phone when they call; maybe that means our product isn't good enough, or it's too expensive, or maybe the economy is really hurting sales. Only the last is an external factor that we may not have immediate control over, but sometimes it is also an excuse. What I want to know is how we can adapt and use changing macro market conditions to our advantage. Correctly measuring what is working individually and collectively is key so that we have an opportunity to stay the course, consider an alternative strategy, or completely change our approach and retrain our salespeople to become more resilient during changing market conditions.

KPIs and Data Analysis

How often should you train or retrain your teams? That's where key performance indicators (KPIs) come into play, because the numbers tell a story. KPIs can also help identify areas that need work and what isn't working. We'll talk more about KPIs in Chapter 5. By creating benchmarks, the gold standard for reps can be measured in an aggregated way that allows comparisons between reps and offices in different parts of the world.

When comparing performance data at every step of the process, erosion of opportunities becomes more obvious. If I'm measuring that, I can identify where the bottleneck is and at what points in the process opportunities are being lost. That, in turn, lets me see that a training process or a retraining to institute best practices is needed. Some aspects rarely need to be trained more than once, while others require continual training.

It's like changing the oil in your car regularly. With some reps, unless someone is listening to their tapes and emphasizing certain things, the wheels start to come off, and they start doing things much more loosely. When you aggregate all these different things that they're not doing as assiduously, you discover a lot of missed opportunities and inefficiencies. So it's crucial to keep them tight through feedback—not everyone can see how they're changing their process in approaching clients on a daily, weekly, or monthly basis.

I sometimes tell people, "You know yourself better than I do, but you can't see under your nose. I can see under your nose. There are things that you can't see that I can see. Let me be your coach, invite me in. Let me tell you what I see."

Having managers who offer the benefit of doubt, who are nonjudgmental and who are not about making people feel badly, is the key to getting people to trust the process and be forthcoming about what's working or not. Sometimes it's not something that's easily observable or hearable. Sometimes a pattern is known by the rep, but they're only going to disclose the information in a safe environment.

Creating a KPI system that reflects what is actually happening on the ground in the sales process is an important exercise, but some companies analyze this in a two-dimensional way. For instance, they might look at the number of calls and talk time, and say, "You're not working hard enough." Whereas other companies might really get granular and say, "Okay, last month, you created one hundred pitch opportunities, fifty of those pitch opportunities were created by emails and LinkedIn, fifty were created by calls. Through your process of targeted messaging, you only got responses to one in twenty of your targeted messages, and the gold standard is one in ten. So let's see how we can improve upon that, and you're only reaching a decision-maker every fifteen times you dial the phone, or twenty times—the gold standard is one in ten. Let's go through that process and see how often you're getting to those prospects. And then, once you get those hundred pitch opportunities set up, how often are you getting to different milestones in the pitch? How often do you get to qualify? How often are you disclosing the price? How often does that lead to a decision that means a second call? And what are the closing percentages?"

Those are just examples of prospecting milestones.

We want to see patterns that are going to allow the right level of intervention and training, and review and retraining, to optimize performance. Once you have a system like that, creating predictable revenue is possible, because I can look at a rep and a sure KPI system to say, "How much money do you want to make next month?" And they can give me a number. If we're really clever on how we measure those data points, and we're aware of what the gold standard is, I can say, "Okay, with your level of performance at each of these steps, this is how many sales opportunities you need to create for the law of averages and numbers to kick in for you to extract that much income this month."

Sometimes people need to know the endgame to really motivate them to put in the work. Sometimes I'll tell someone, "Look, based on your numbers, you're not going to achieve this unless you work twenty-four hours a day. Or you can work smart so that you're not wasting time on things that matter less to create more opportunities to achieve your goals.

When I first started selling, we didn't have enough data, so we focused mostly on looking for silly patterns. It was not optimized at all. With one rep, what kept her going was she knew that she would make a sale with every ninety-ninth CEO she spoke to. So she would start smelling it after ninety conversations, and then, lo and behold, within one or two of ninety-nine, she would close a deal. I've seen people be superstitious and countdown in strange ways. In some aspects, it was the Wild West when I started in sales. We only tracked the number of calls and how much time people were on the phone, and sales were much less predictable because we were just so limited in our ability to forecast that.

Under such conditions, you may be turning over a lot more reps, which costs a lot of money. That's where people are losing faith because they never see the light at the end of the tunnel. Whereas, with KPIs, you can tell people you're almost there because you can see how they've grown their performance over time. You can graph it or track it or slice and dice the data in many different ways, especially with modern CRM systems, which you can program in any way you want to look at the pie. It provides the technology to be able to optimize sales;

predictability around sales is now available to us. That's one of the themes of this book.

Review Process

The review process is a key tool for creating continuous growth in a high-performance sales team. Other useful tools are process training, tape training, planning meetings, and strategy sessions. The review process is an opportunity to look at what's been done, what's working at the highest level of performance, what isn't working, and then identifying the weaknesses and making a plan for turning those weaknesses into strengths. This is a process that relies on data, not just in terms of things like sales numbers, but for breaking down what the sales process is, looking at everything from lead generation to pitch opportunities, to different milestones in the prospecting and pitching process—achieving those as well as getting to a point of conversion.

I would say that all salespeople require a review at least once a month. Sometimes, if things are not going well, a two-week milestone is warranted. There are times, probably, when it's so critical and dire that it's worth spending some time every week. I would say monthly and quarterly reviews are important and serve specific purposes. Then, obviously, six-month reviews and annual reviews. All have a different purpose and different levels of specificity, but all are about catching problems early and being able to identify weaknesses and then coming up with a plan for turning those weaknesses into strengths.

When someone is doing the same thing erroneously for weeks or months, it's a missed opportunity. If it's not noticed, and you realize what it is after the fact, it is painful to discover that if it had just been reviewed earlier, it could have been corrected.

Monthly reviews have to do with hitting monthly goals, assessing what's happening on a day-to-day or weekly basis and how that corresponds to where one needs to be. The quarterly review might take into account the averages—so, if someone had two good months and one bad month, we can try to reduce those ups and downs. With the six-month review, probably something similar, but on a slightly different scale or focus. Then the annual review is not only to align the salespeople with their contribution to the sales team and the sales organization and the company at large but also to make sure that they're pulling their weight or being recognized for driving a new standard.

Review processes can be used to recognize and reward high-performing sales team members by setting new bars, and by identifying stretch targets and stretch objectives.

Because people are motivated by different things, it's important to analyze the dialogue that occurs during the review process to understand what's going to motivate reps. This can then be used to create incentives that will help them achieve better versions, or accelerated versions, of their sales performance.

Many companies have built high-performance sales teams that have helped them become some of the leading companies in the world. Salesforce has a great sales culture, and a lot of that stems from them building a high-performance culture—same for HubSpot. Google is another example, as well as Cisco, LinkedIn, and Nuance. These are really good companies that have used high-performance sales teams as a way of driving them into the upper echelons.

CHAPTER 5
Making Sales Predictable

Many companies use KPIs extensively to drive sales performance. IBM, for example, focuses on metrics such as sales pipeline conversion rates, average contract value, sales cycle lengths, and customer acquisition costs to evaluate their sales effectiveness. They leverage data-driven insights to identify trends, forecast sales opportunities, and make strategic decisions that optimize their sales efforts.

In this chapter, we'll focus on how to add predictability to sales using metrics such as KPIs (key performance indicators) and benchmarking. We'll also cover reverse engineering results and making nimble adjustments. Readers interested in diving deep into the weeds of sales metrics and the associated data analysis will find food for thought in the following pages.

Creating a KPI system

KPIs can be used to improve sales predictability in a variety of ways. One method is *identifying trends*. By tracking sales over time, we can identify patterns in the sales data. This can help forecast future sales more accurately. It can also be used for *measuring performance* against specific goals and targets, which can help identify areas where we need to improve and adjust our sales strategy.

Another function of KPIs is to help *predict sales outcomes*. By analyzing historical sales data KPIs, sales teams can make predictions about future sales outcomes, and adjust their sales strategy to meet future demand. *Forecasting revenue* can be accomplished by using KPIs such as conversion rate averages for order value or sales value or customer acquisition cost sales.

This can help sales teams set realistic sales targets and make informed decisions around resource allocations.

There are many examples of successful implementations of a data-driven sales strategy. At one point, Walmart made a lot of data-driven changes to its supply chain that impacted a variety of factors that helped to drive sales and increase revenues. The company was able to reduce out-of-stock items by a measurable amount, leading to an increase in revenue. Much of this was accomplished through data analytics of their operations, and having that translate into greater sales.

Amazon has also taken advantage of this approach, and they now have a recommendation engine that probably accounts for in the area of 35 percent of the company's sales by automating and profiling customers, and recommending products and upselling.

A great example from our business, which I mentioned earlier in the book, resulted from some observations early in the pandemic and how we were able, as a company that organizes face-to-face matchmaking opportunities between buyers and sellers at five-star resorts, to adapt our approach to the circumstances. Using data to understand who was doing what well allowed us to allocate resources appropriately, and to identify who could actually create revenue the traditional way and who couldn't in those tougher market conditions and how we could mobilize those people.

We were able to use the time savings that our best people had achieved to fill their calendars and get them prospecting more than they would have using the traditional approach, which led to an increase in sales overall. It was data that allowed us to identify this early and helped us make that pivot to take advantage of unprecedented and rapidly changing market conditions.

To ensure that the data being collected is accurate and reliable, it's important to use rigorous data collection methods. That requires planning, thought, and research. You also want to make sure to collect sufficient data—you don't want to be making changes based on a sample of one or two. Additionally, make sure to clean and validate data. If someone has a rash, you don't want to amputate their leg—miscalculations can happen if you use incorrect data.

Also, it's important to use analytics tools to understand outliers and anomalies—that's possible with the right technology and CRMs to continually monitor and update data.

A question that often arises is how sales leaders can effectively communicate the importance of data-driven decision-making to their teams. This is similar to other change management exercises, but depending on the extent pragmatic sales teams individually and collectively can be inspired by the upside of potential outcomes, getting them to buy in can be encouraged through the following four steps:

1. Explain the benefit.
2. Provide training.
3. Encourage collaboration.
4. Lead by example.

KPIs should be reviewed and adjusted regularly, whatever that means to your organization. It depends on several factors, such as whether business goals are changing rapidly, in which case the KPIs need to change at a similar pace. The same with industry trends.

Additionally, if a KPI consistently falls short of a target, it may be necessary to adjust the target itself. Operational changes can also impact KPI performance and necessitate a review. External factors such as economic conditions, regulatory changes, and geopolitical events can also affect KPI performance.

To ensure that the KPIs are aligned with broader company objectives and incentivize the right behaviors in sales teams, you can take a number of steps.

One is to *align objectives*. Start with the company objectives and make sure the KPIs match the broader objectives. Defining the company's objectives first and then mapping out the KPIs to help achieve these objectives is the first step in that process. It's also important to *involve sales teams in KPI development*. They are the ones who are going to help identify the factors that are leading to more or fewer sales. Getting their input helps ensure their buy-in and commitment.

Use SMART criteria. Ensure that KPIs are specific, measurable, achievable, relevant, and time-bound. In short, ensure that KPIs are aligned with the company objectives and provide the right incentives for the sales teams. To incentivize the right behaviors, *align KPIs with compensation* to ensure that if you're trying to improve a point of performance, you're linking compensation or commission or bonuses or other incentives to achieving those points.

Measure and track KPIs regularly to help identify where teams are excelling or falling short, enabling adjustments to be made sooner rather than later. Also, *provide feedback and coaching to sales teams on* KPI *performances* to help them understand how they are performing and identify areas where they can improve. *Communicate KPIs effectively* and ensure that sales teams understand the KPIs and how they relate to the broader company objectives.

I tell my managers that if they hire someone, it's their responsibility to keep them on track, and if that individual goes off track, they need to do something. Holding managers accountable for the performance of the people who they choose to put on their teams is essential, not just letting them wash their hands and say, "I want somebody else." As far as I'm concerned, that's a dereliction of their responsibility.

It's important to balance the need for KPIs with other factors that may impact sales performance, such as external market conditions or product quality. Key to accomplishing this is having a sense of perspective about the impact of external factors and, if necessary, to adjust KPIs in response. It can be helpful to use a balanced scorecard approach with KPIs that use both financial and nonfinancial factors. This lets you gain a more comprehensive view of sales performance and account for external market conditions and product quality. It also makes sense to consider both leading and lagging indicators—the lead indicators help identify trends of potential issues before they impact sales performance, whereas lagging indicators can provide insight into the impact of external factors on sales performance.

KPIs are one of the key mechanisms we have today to make revenue predictable and to find ways to make it grow. If you're smart about it, there's a story in all these data points that can help any business make better decisions.

Benchmarking Performance

I define benchmarking as the practice of comparing your sales performance and processes with those of other sales teams, offices, internal divisions, or businesses in your industry or market. It involves identifying best practices, performance standards, and other metrics that help you measure your own performance and identify areas of improvement. It's important for sales for a few reasons.

First, it helps you identify realistic goals and targets for your own sales team. It is also useful in identifying best practices that you may be able to adopt to improve your own sales performance.

Benchmarking can also help in improving processes by identifying areas where your sales process may be falling short and where you can make improvements to become more efficient and effective. Another benefit is that it can help you stay competitive by ensuring you're keeping up with industry standards and trends.

To identify the right benchmarks for your sales team, start by identifying the industry or market in which the business operates. This helps determine the relevant benchmarking criteria and other businesses that you should be comparing yourself to. Then analyze the sales data to identify where you are lagging behind other teams and businesses, and identify areas where you are performing well. This will help determine which benchmarks are most relevant to the team. It's also important to identify competitors, especially those that are outperforming you. This will help you set realistic goals and determine which areas you need to focus on improving.

Once you have identified the right benchmark and set goals, monitor your progress and make adjustments as needed to help stay on track and meet your goals.

To measure and track performance against benchmarks in your market, it's important to understand when you are comparing apples to oranges, and the differences as well as the commonalities when comparing them. You might have a company that's emphasizing an end user strategy to drive sales or another that's more about getting face-to-face meetings and fanatical prospecting. Those broad approaches are going to reveal different stories.

In this world, many businesses are going to set themselves up so that they are slightly different from everyone else, either in delivery or some particular feature i.e., niche-crafting as noted in Chapter 1. Pure benchmarking, in that case, may be difficult, because there may be some variables that cannot be controlled or isolated, but that could also be taken into consideration. There is really a lot of human analysis that goes into considering, "Okay, there are three possibilities taking place here, and it's either A, B, or C. Let's come up with a plan for all three, and then see which one is best, or if that analysis yields any other patterns."

I think that trial-and-error and A/B testing are such a fundamental part of getting people within the ballpark, because you have to start somewhere, and sometimes the possibilities are so broad that you have to take some chances in what you're testing to see if a pattern emerges.

Some common benchmarks used in sales include these:

- ❖ Sales revenue
- ❖ Sales growth
- ❖ Conversion rate
- ❖ Average deal size
- ❖ Sales cycle
- ❖ Customer acquisition cost
- ❖ Customer lifetime value (CLV)

Benchmarks should be reviewed regularly to ensure that they remain relevant and accurate. Some benchmarks should be reviewed on a monthly or quarterly basis while others should be reviewed annually. Because the KPIs are really that granular, they can provide an understanding of what's happening on a day-to-day basis. Regular benchmark reviews can help identify areas for improvement and opportunities for growth to help businesses remain competitive with their sales performance over time.

It is a lot of work, and it requires a lot of attention. There are so many temptations in business to go by "gut feel." While there is a place for that, if it's not done in a complementary way with more scientific approaches, it can be counterproductive. Sometimes people will change ten things, and nine of them were already right, and one of them was wrong, and it throws everything off balance. Comparatively, the idea of making isolated adjustments, testing them and looking for patterns is more sound, but it can take time.

I'm like a bumblebee going from one flower collecting nectar and pollen when I travel from city to city doing office visits. But instead, I gather information. I've used benchmarking many times between offices and can supercharge the process of aligning best practices by analyzing and observing comparatively what and how things are being done, and what the consistent and inconsistent variables are. It's always a matter of following the frontrunner and pulling up the socks of the organization that's lagging, and then looking for the patterns through data and interviews, as well as just normal analysis, to find weaknesses.

One weakness that I found in an office was when we, post-pandemic, started tracking certain KPIs across offices using a uniform system I put in place. We really didn't know what a good performance was when it came to certain forms of prospecting by email, certain forms of prospecting by LinkedIn, or calling. I went to one office in Toronto, and I found one salesperson who had response rates that were through the roof. She could get people to engage through email at rates of 15 to 20 percent. I dissected the things that she was doing differently, such as clever subject lines, strategic name drops, and enticing calls to action motivating prospects to reply more frequently. It was very time-consuming, but the engagement was undeniably powerful.

Then when I went to an office in Europe that I hadn't visited in a while, I saw that some people were creating opportunities at 2 to 5 percent, and this hadn't been improved or even caught by the people on the ground. So we completely revamped the system and set a standard where people needed to be above 10 percent. That actually drove a lot of change in getting some of the people in the office prospecting more directly by reaching out by telephone or other communication avenues rather than relying on email or LinkedIn because those just weren't working. It also led to revamping excessively lengthy messages. That improved the performance of the people who continued in that office dramatically—all of a sudden, some were going from 2 to 5 percent to about 10 percent.

I'm using an example of inter-office benchmarking, but some companies might have to benchmark with their competitors, depending on what information is available. Both are similar because each office operates in a certain ecosystem that needs to be understood in comparison with other ecosystems that are performing a similar function.

Reverse Engineering Results

Reverse engineering results is a term that I started using a while ago without any real theory behind it. I look at it like this: there are patterns where we can predict the future; if the process is pure, the outcomes and the outputs are pure. If the measures along the way adhere to a certain standard, I can get to the point in the review where I can ask someone how much money they want to make or how much success they want to have, and I can reverse engineer it based on the gold standard of KPIs and say, "Okay, if you did this much work and have this pace of work, you will generate this amount of income."

In the same way, someone who's running a marathon could be told, "If you're at this point at 10k, and you're at this point at 20k, this is going to be the result if you finish strong."

Reverse engineering results means analyzing the end results of successful sales or business transactions by working backward to identify the steps that led to that outcome. The approach involves breaking down the sales process into smaller sections and examining each step to understand what worked and what didn't. This can help sales teams identify patterns, strategies, and tactics that can be replicated to achieve similar results. The approach can also help them identify areas where they need to adjust their strategies to improve their sales.

The following are steps that can be used in the process of reverse engineering sales results:

1. Define sales goals.
2. Identify current sales results.
3. Analyze the sales process.
4. Identify key performance indicators.
5. Compare KPIs to benchmarks.

6. Identify gaps and opportunities.
7. Develop an action plan.
8. Monitor and adjust.

There are many reasons why a sales team should reverse engineer their results. For one, it can help *replicate success*. There's always an opportunity to do a postmortem and dissect all the elements that went into making a sale successful. By reverse engineering the steps that led to this successful sale, the team can identify the strategies and tactics that worked and replicate them in future sales. It can also help *improve performance by analyzing the steps that led to unsuccessful sales results*. Teams can identify areas where they need to improve their performance to help them adjust their strategies and tactics to achieve better results in future sales.

Reverse engineering can help teams *adapt to changing marketing conditions* by identifying trends and shifts in the market and adjusting sales strategies accordingly. Again, this comes with the disclaimer that you can't be flip-flopping on a sample of one or two—trends need to be true and statistically significant—and there are ways of ensuring that the tail isn't wagging the dog when it comes to such changes. Reverse engineering can also *optimize sales performance by breaking down the sales process into smaller parts*, enabling sales teams to identify areas where they can streamline their process and improve efficiency.

It's also important to ensure that you're not just looking at surface-level metrics, but actually getting to the root cause of any issue. Look for patterns and correlations in the data between different metrics—this will help identify the cause of the problem. Talk to sales reps, customers, and other stakeholders to get their perspective on the issue to get more insights. Test and develop hypotheses based on the data to see if they are valid; use A/B testing or other methods to validate the hypotheses.

Once you've identified the root cause, make sure to address it. Then implement changes to the sales process, such as training programs and other strategies needed to improve performance.

The following are tools and techniques that can be used for effective reverse engineering of sales results:

- ❖ Sales data analytics tools
- ❖ Customer relationship management (CRM) software
- ❖ Sales process mapping to help identify bottlenecks and efficiencies and areas of improvement
- ❖ A/B testing of two or more variations of the sales process to see which one performs better

(We'll address A/B testing more extensively in the next chapter.)

Isolated and Nimble Adjustments

Isolated adjustments focus on specific aspects of sales performance and aim to single out the impact of an aspect on overall sales results. For instance, if a company wants to see how much impact a particular marketing campaign had on sales, they might compare sales results before and after its implementation.

By isolating the campaign, by keeping all other controllable variables the same, they get a clear picture of its impact on sales without the influence of other factors. Focusing on nimble adjustments feeds into the whole idea of small data and observations that we're going to discuss in the next chapter There are big factors that require a lot of analysis, and there are nimble adjustments and small observations that need to be identified and measured.

Once those nimble adjustments are isolated, anyone can analyze the results and talk through what could be having an impact, and then potentially A/B test it. All of these mechanisms fit together, at least to some degree, but you never want to work with non-isolated adjustments—for example, by making five different changes simultaneously and then trying to understand the impact. Four of them might have been right and only one wrong, but you'll never know which because you're changing things that are working.

In the case of isolated adjustments, comparative analysis could help companies distinguish the impact of any specific factor on sales performance. If a company wants to launch a new product, they can compare sales results before and after the launch, similar to the marketing campaign.

In the case of a nimble adjustment, if sales have declined in a particular month, comparative analysis can help companies determine if the decrease is due to fewer working days or a major holiday. Comparative analysis is a crucial tool in making isolated and nimble adjustments relevant to sales.

Recently, we realized that some of the industries we were involved with could not support the price we had set. In brief, the volume that we had chosen to sell at and the level of financial commitment that they had to demonstrate to become a customer weren't working as well as in the past. Simply experimenting by cutting the volume in half and giving them half the product for approximately half the price, more of a crawl-walk-run approach, helped drive sales in a few industries that were a little bit more price-sensitive than others. That's an example of a successful experiment that worked in three specific industries. It allowed us to discover that it wasn't the cost per unit but the gross cost that was reducing the number of relationships compared to other industries.

To ensure that adjustments made based on comparative analysis are effective and sustainable, I recommend taking the following steps:

1. Define the problem clearly.
2. Collect relevant data.

3. Use appropriate statistical methods.
4. Test the effectiveness of the adjustment.
5. Continually monitor and adjust.

Employing and balancing the need for isolated and nimble adjustments with the need for a consistent sales strategy can be challenging for people who are creatures of habit. I've worked with a few individuals who took a really long time, even with good advice, to change course. Then I've met other people who will take a sample, a really logical sample, test it ten times, and decide to stay with it a little longer or abandon it, based on an almost scientific approach.

I would even argue that some of the best salespeople are the best because they make sensible changes quickly based on small but relevant samples. This is as opposed to them being better communicators, better at follow-up, or better at sales process. That's because if you can make your mistakes quickly and early and change course and not get stuck, that could influence a whole month, a whole quarter, and a whole year.

CHAPTER 6

An Evolving Sales Strategy

An evolving sales strategy is important in today's business environment because the sales landscape is constantly changing, requiring a willingness to adjust practices to stay competitive. As technology advances, customers are becoming savvier and empowered. They have access to more information than ever before and expect personalized experiences.

It's a competitive market out there. New technologies are emerging all the time, and businesses that don't adapt risk falling behind. An evolving sales strategy can help them align their sales efforts with their changing goals. Change seems to be accelerating from one year to the next, and I think that, if anything, the need to adapt—to be willing to change—is only going to gain momentum.

Kodak was founded in 1888. The company was so dominant for nearly one hundred years that by 1976, 85 percent of all film cameras and 90 percent of all film sold in the US was Kodak. In 1975, a Kodak engineer invented the first digital camera, but Kodak executives failed to recognize the potential of digital photography, and the speed at which digital photography would take over a market traditionally dominated by film.

The company had a culture that focused on protecting its traditional film business, which hindered its ability to adapt quickly to changing market dynamics This resistance to change prevented Kodak from capitalizing on emerging opportunities in the digital photography market; instead, Kodak continued to heavily invest in film, which eventually became a declining business.

Kodak filed for bankruptcy on January 12, 2012, and re-emerged in 2013 as a company focused on commercial printing and packaging solutions. In so doing, the company had given up its position as the market leader in consumer photography because of an inability to adjust with innovation and correctly evolve over time.

Implementing an evolving sales strategy can create challenges. One of the foremost is *resistance to change*. It typically takes effort and commitment to make changes stick, as discussed in the last chapter. As a result, it's important to communicate the benefits of modifications to the sales strategy and provide training to help employees adapt.

Another challenge is *lack of data*. Well-designed sales strategies often rely on data to identify the optimal decision. If a business doesn't have access to the right data, it can be difficult to amend an effective strategy. *Integration issues* can also cause difficulties. An evolving sales strategy may require integration with other systems or processes, which can be complex and time-consuming.

Resource constraints can pose another challenge. Implementing a complete sales strategy may require additional resources such as technology or personnel, which can be a stretch for businesses with limited budgets. Another issue is *balancing short and long-term goals*. An evolving sales strategy may require short-term sacrifices for long-term gains. It's important to find a balance between immediate sales goals and long-term business objectives.

Given these challenges, how can you ensure that an evolving sales strategy remains aligned with the business's overall objectives and goals? The following steps can help you achieve this objective:

1. Set clear business objectives.
2. Align sales strategy with business objectives.
3. Monitor sales performance.
4. Communicate and collaborate with teams and stakeholders.

A/B Testing

A/B testing is also known as split testing. It's a technique used to compare two versions of a sales strategy to determine which one performs better. It involves two variants of the sales strategy that are identical except for one or two variables. These variables could be the color of a button, the wording of a call to action, the layout of the page, and so on. I have a friend who worked in a business where he had to generate clicks online. One tactic they used was to flash one picture with a woman and another picture of the same woman with sunglasses to see the results produced by the sunglasses.

The two versions in the A/B test are shown to two different groups of customers with similar demographic profiles, or otherwise measured in a scientific fashion, and the performance of each version is compared. The version that performs better is considered the winner. The other version is discarded. This process is repeated with different variables until the best-performing version is identified.

A/B testing is used in sales to optimize sales strategies and improve conversion rates. By identifying the most effective variables, businesses can refine their sales strategies and increase sales. It's a valuable tool for businesses looking to improve sales performance and stay competitive in the market.

Conducting A/B tests has a number of benefits. Among the most important are *improved conversion rates*. A/B testing allows businesses to identify the best-performing version of their sales materials, such as product pages, landing pages, and emails. By optimizing these materials, businesses can improve their conversion rates and generate more sales.

Another benefit can be *reduced bounce rates*. A bounce rate measures how many visitors to a website quickly leave—bounce away from—the site. By identifying elements that are turning potential customers away, businesses can make changes to these elements, helping keep visitors on their site and increasing the chances of making a sale.

A/B testing can also help *boost customer engagement*. Testing different versions of sales materials can help businesses identify elements that resonate with the most customers to boost customer engagement and build strong relationships with their audience. The process can also help *save time and money* by testing different versions of sales materials.

I read one case study of a successful A/B test involving a company that sells online courses that wanted to increase sales. They conducted an A/B test on their checkout page. They wanted to test two versions—one with a one-step checkout process, the other with a multistep process. After running the test, they found that the one-step version resulted in a 10 percent increase in sales compared to the multistep one. This was a significant improvement.

There are five steps to determining which elements or variables to test in an A/B testing scenario:

1. Identify goals.
2. Analyze the data.
3. Conduct user research.
4. Prioritize elements based on goals, data analysis, and user research.
5. Conduct A/B testing on the identified elements and analyze the results.

One of the common pitfalls or challenges to be aware of when conducting A/B testing for sales is *insufficient sample size*. A common mistake is to test a sample size that is too small and draw statistically significant conclusions from it, leading to inaccurate results and misguided decisions. Quite frankly, I see this all the time. Everyone thinks they're observing the right patterns, but oftentimes they're pushing an agenda or misinterpreting too small a sample.

Another danger to avoid is *testing too many variables* in too short a period of time. Doing so can lead to confusing results, making it difficult to determine which changes are responsible for an increase or decrease in sales. This goes back to the isolated and nimble changes we discussed previously.

Yet another challenge can arise from *not defining success metrics*, which makes it difficult to determine whether a test was successful or not. *Ignoring customer feedback* can also be a problem. Customer feedback and preferences should be considered when making changes to the sales strategy; ignoring this feedback can lead to unsuccessful tests and lost sales. Another mistake is not considering the impact of *external factors*, such as seasonality, changes in the market, and promotions, which can all influence the results of an A/B test.

Small Data Observations

"Small data" refers to manageable amounts of information that can be easily analyzed and interpreted to gain insights for decision-making. In the context of sales, small data can include statistics such as consumer demographics, purchase history, and sales figures from a specific period. By contrast, "big data" refers to a large complex dataset that cannot easily be managed or analyzed using traditional data processing tools. In the context of sales, big data can include information from various sources such as social media, online browsing, and customer behavior feedback.

In sales, small data can be useful in identifying trends, patterns, and customer behavior, while big data can help businesses gain deeper understanding of their customers' needs and preferences. Both small and big data can be valuable for sales teams, and the key is to use the right tools and techniques to analyze and interpret the information.

Learning to interpret this type of data takes training. We are a species that has a natural tendency to recognize patterns, which is perhaps how the ancient Greeks figured out the world was round when they saw the same stars passing by at the same time every year. Anyone who has an eye for identifying patterns—once they have the basic methodologies down—will notice things that are happening from one sales opportunity to the next or from one week to the next. You have to pay attention to them and consider what could be causing them. That's what we're talking about in its simplest form while, at a more complex level, we're getting into some things that are harder to recognize with the naked eye.

> **"Where Big Data is all about drawing correlations, Small Data is about identifying causation."**
>
> Martin Lindstrom, *Small Data: The Tiny Clues That Uncover Huge Trends*

There are several ways small data observations can be valuable in understanding customer behavior and improving sales strategies:

- ❖ Identifying customer needs and preferences
- ❖ Revealing trends and patterns in consumer behavior
- ❖ Personalizing marketing efforts
- ❖ Identifying opportunities from emerging trends
- ❖ Targeting specific demographics

❖ Improving the customer service experience

For example, a small data observation influenced a significant change in our approach to basic sales process differentiation. In this case, we noticed that we had a group of salespeople who would create value in a customer presentation, then set a follow-up call involving their manager or a trained closer to complete the sale. Some groups—or some salespeople—were really successful at that, having the second call take place 75 percent of the time, and others were weak, only converting 25 percent of the time while using the same fundamental sales process.

By getting granular about some of the decisions being made, we discovered that the process used to set up the second call could be broken up into a series of steps, and marginal adjustments to that process made a massive difference in the closing percentages. This highlighted several strong differences we were able to impart to our salespeople, such as leaving the prospect wanting more by holding back information, defining a hook or purpose for the next call. and instead of pushing for the callback make it their idea. Such tweaks made a huge difference—most likely by leaving prospects wanting more and more inclined to turn up at the agreed time.

There are potential limitations or challenges to relying on small data for decision-making in sales. Five issues are particularly salient.

First is *limited sample size*. That's a bit of an oxymoron because while we don't want a trend of just two or three, a sample is by definition limited. Since we're looking for patterns, though, it's about finding a balance. Small data typically involves a limited sample size that can, if not carefully scrutinized, lead to bias or inaccurate results, as a small sample may not be representative of a pattern. I see this all the time—people flip-flopping and changing processes because of an abstruse small sample size and getting it wrong and having to backtrack.

The second challenge is *lack of diversity*. If small data do not capture a full range of customer behaviors or preferences or patterns in the sales process, it could result in a narrow perspective on sales performance, which could restrict the company's capacity to identify new opportunities or optimize sales strategies.

Third is *limited granularity*. Small data may not provide the level of detail needed to identify specific trends or patterns of customer behavior, and this can make it difficult to identify root causes of sales performance issues or to fine-tune sales strategies.

Fourth is *time-consuming analysis*. Data may require more time and effort to analyze, and larger data sets may be needed as the insights may not be immediately apparent. This can be challenging for organizations that need to make quick decisions based on sales performance. This is also a challenge associated with big data.

The fifth challenge is *difficulty in generating insights*. Small data may not be generalizable to other contexts or markets, making it difficult to apply insights from one dataset to another.

Please note that while these are the limitations of small data sets, they are also sometimes the benefits.

A variety of tools and techniques can be used to effectively capture and analyze small data in a sales setting. A *CRM* can help collect and organize the data, which can be used to identify patterns and trends to inform sales strategy. *Surveys and feedback forms* can be used to gather information insights for sales strategies: simple surveys can be conducted by email or social media to customers, while more detailed surveys can be done in person or over the phone.

Social media monitoring is another method of accessing and analyzing small data. Tools like Hootsuite and Sprout Social can be used to monitor social media activity. *Sales analytic tools* such as Tableau or Salesforce analytics can help visualize sales data and identify trends and patterns and be used to connect predictive analysis and help forecast future sales trends. *Data visualization tools* such as Infogram and Canva can help create visual representations of sales data, making it easier to understand and communicate with stakeholders. *Data analysis techniques* such as regression analysis can also be useful.

A book I read that really took me down the rabbit hole on the subject of small data is, appropriately, *Small Data*, by Martin Lindstrom. It contains stories and anecdotes demonstrating the power of small data observations, one of which was about him helping to fix Lego when the company was in danger of going out of business. Lego's marketing research team turned around the company's fortunes simply by noticing the scuff patterns on the shoe of a German skateboarder teenager. At the time, Lego's strategy was to shift from smaller pieces to bigger pieces, and this was the company's response to the threat of children wanting to play video games instead of Lego. Observations from the German skateboard teenager's shoe, from doing ollies and other tricks, led to the conclusion that, as Lindstrom put it, "children attain social currency among their peers by playing and achieving a high level of mastery at their chosen skill, whatever that skill happens to be." The scuff pattern showed a level of proficiency in the teenager's skateboarding skills that was recognized by his peers.

This small data observation caused Lego to reverse course on its bigger piece strategy and develop a strategy encouraging Lego consumers to build famous structures, such as the Taj Mahal or the Empire State Building, making recognition among their peers a benefit of mastering and completing a Lego project.

Since then, Lego has grown to again become one of the largest toy companies in the world, after having flirted with bankruptcy before this change in strategy. Small data observations can be as subtle yet important as that.

Shifting Market Conditions

Shifting market conditions and trends relate to changes in the business environment that impact the sales process. These changes can be driven by various factors, including changes in customer preferences, advancements in technologies, shifts in the competitive landscape, or changes in the regulatory environment.

As an example, there have been huge shifts in recent years toward eco-friendly products. Companies that have responded to that trend have been able to increase sales and gain competitive advantages, and that applies in a B2B environment as well. I see many examples from situations where we introduced investors to money managers who can grow and preserve their wealth. First in Europe and then in the United States, many investors had a huge appetite for impact investments—generally, eco-friendly or other investments that are going to do the world good—and that's the differentiator when it comes to where they want to invest their money.

For observant salespeople, some common indicators or signals suggest market conditions are changing. These include the following:

- ❖ Changes in customer behavior
- ❖ Competitor activity
- ❖ Economic indicators
- ❖ Technological advancement
- ❖ Regulatory changes
- ❖ Customer feedback

It's critical for sales professionals to stay updated on market trends. I often ask people, "What are you reading? What are you looking at to stay ahead of things?" That's just part of the ongoing job of sales professionals because you will get left in the dark if you are not evolving. I've seen this throughout the years. Things that we might have been doing five years ago—even though the process is fundamentally the same or the targets are the same—just wouldn't work now, and it's all evolved organically through small adjustments day after day, week after week, month after month, year after year. When you assemble it all five years later, it's a very different animal.

COVID-19 is an example of a recent market shift or trend that significantly impacted sales strategies or approaches across many industries. Because of lockdowns and social distancing measures, sales professionals had to pivot into virtual sales and remote work. This led to increased use of online channels and sales tools and a greater focus on customer support.

Another example is the rise of influencer marketing, which has impacted sales strategies across many industries. I know one money manager who focuses on influencer marketing, partnering with individuals or celebrities with a substantial presence on social media. Any one of these people could just announce a new product line on their social media and easily generate millions of impressions, and instant sales. The power of that is incredible, and this didn't exist ten years ago.

I would also cite the e-commerce boom. The growth of e-commerce has impacted sales strategies in many industries, including retail. It's funny. Sometimes I see sales processes that I use show up in my social media interactions. As described in an earlier chapter, one day, a men's shoe popped up on my screen, and I thought, *Oh, those are amazing Dior loafers…* And then I got so engaged that I went to search my size, and they said, "Sold out." All of a sudden, it created this burning desire; then three days later, it popped up again and said, "We have them in stock," and I bought them straight away.

In retrospect, I needed to realize what it felt like not to have the opportunity to buy the shoes and feel an emotional loss before I realized I actually wanted the shoes enough to make a purchasing commitment. Stated simply, that's what sales is all about.

Salespeople need to be adaptable or willing to change their approach based on shifting market conditions, and companies may need to develop new products or services or adopt new sales channels, or adjust pricing strategy. They also need to embrace technology and leverage it to their advantage.

I remember the first person who sent me a LinkedIn invite around twenty years ago. I thought to myself, *What is this LinkedIn?* You have to be open-minded to get in the game because you never know where technology is going to go. There are many, many examples of salespeople who have been reluctant to use novel sales tools, and in a matter of months or years, they are so far behind that it's very difficult to catch up.

It's also important to focus on building relationships. While marketing conditions may shift, the importance of building strong relationships remains constant. Prioritizing relationship building can help insulate salespeople from those shifts and allow enough time to adapt.

A fascinating example of successfully adapting to shifting market conditions was the introduction, about a decade ago, of webinars as a service by our company, in addition to traditional events that had been fundamental to our product lineup. There was an emerging presence of webinars in the marketplace that seemed to be selling at lower price points than we would usually consider. Because we had such a robust database, it gave us an opportunity to come up with curated webinars that served as a mechanism for our clients to qualify prospective customers through comparative analysis. Our curated webinars had more value, especially when combined with our other services that allowed face-to-face meeting introductions with those customers, with a higher probability of closing. It really involved a shift in our thinking to open our minds to the possibility that adding webinars to our product lineup could not only create steady revenues but could also allow our traditional products to work even better for some clients.

As discussed previously, when the pandemic hit and people couldn't meet face-to-face or participate in our normal product lines, everyone wanted one of these curated webinars or online events. They still needed to get in front of their customers. We had a perfect way to make that happen in the intermediate period before we started offering meetings online through Zoom VC. I think it's a very relevant story, because it all started with being open to something that we would have previously resisted, and how it really became valuable when market conditions shifted dramatically as a result of the pandemic.

CHAPTER 7
Working Hard

Fanatical prospecting is the practice of consistently and persistently reaching out to potential customers to generate new business. The term, which was popularized in a book called *Fanatical Prospecting* by James Blount, involves identifying and targeting potential leads and then using various communication channels such as phone, email, and social media to engage with them to turn them into paying customers.

Fanatical prospecting in the sales industry is important because the key driver of revenue growth is new customers. Without a steady stream of new customers, businesses can struggle to maintain their sales figures and may eventually stagnate or decline.

By contrast, companies that prioritize prospecting and invest in building effective sales pipelines are more likely to see sustained growth and success, which also helps sales. Sales professionals build strong relationships with their existing customers by staying in touch with potential leads, keeping them engaged over time, which can ultimately lead to more sales and referrals.

Oracle is renowned for its highly driven and hardworking sales team. The company has a culture of setting ambitious goals and expects its salespeople to put in the effort required to meet and exceed these objectives. Oracle salespeople are known for their dedication, resilience, and willingness to go the extra mile to close deals.

Sales strategies allow companies to absorb their eroding client base, because most companies are not capable of maintaining 100 percent client retention and because growth is simply a formula between how many customers you are losing every year, how many you are retaining, and how many you are adding.

If you're retaining 80 percent, you need to replace that 20 percent and add new customers to create growth. Just like an evaporating lake that requires both rain and streams bringing replacement water to sustain itself, business can evaporate as well. It's important to get ahead of that curve.

Prospecting Strategies and Techniques

Companies can choose from a variety of key strategies or techniques that successful sales professionals utilize for effective prospecting. These include the following:

- ❖ **Research and qualified prospect targeting**. Research and identify ideal customer profiles and use data analytics to understand target market demographics and interest behaviors.
- ❖ **Multichannel outreach**. Prospecting isn't just about phone calls and emails. Sales reps can use a variety of communication channels such as social media, video calls, and even direct mail to reach potential customers.
- ❖ **Sales automation tools**. CRM software, sales engagement platforms, etc., can help salespeople streamline their prospecting efforts, automate outreach, and track engagements.
- ❖ **Personalization**. Take time to understand the customer's pain points and their needs to tailor communications for follow-up.
- ❖ **Consistent follow-up**. Sales professionals follow up, plan, and schedule to ensure that they are staying

on top of their prospecting while building ongoing relationships.

❖ **Referral programs**. Referrals are a good way to leverage existing customers to generate new leads.

It's important to strike a balance between quantity and quality when it comes to prospecting by having a follow-up plan and using data analysis to find which prospecting method is yielding the best results. This does tie into data as well, which I'll cover later in the chapter. Before you start prospecting, find your ideal customer profile to ensure that you're approaching the right prospects—this will help you focus on quality over quantity so you're not wasting time on prospects that are not a good fit. You can use data analytics to identify best practices and prioritize them based on their likelihood to convert. Look for patterns in the data to help in this process.

Focus your efforts on high-quality leads. For example, look for core prospects that meet all the fundamental criteria of an ideal client versus fringe prospects, who meet only some of the characteristics. With the latter, it will likely be more difficult to engage someone. As such, these types of prospects might close at percentages far less often than core prospects. The extent of the variation in closing between various levels of prospect qualification can often be determined through data and data analytics.

Prospecting Challenges and Measuring Success

Many different challenges or roadblocks confront salespeople when implementing a fanatical prospecting approach. The first is *lack of discipline*. This is always one of the biggest challenges. Selling takes drive and purpose—consistency is key to success in sales.

To overcome this challenge, it's important to establish a routine—a dedicated time each day for prospecting. I recently went through this with one of my offices, where we did a time management plan based on Stephen Covey's *7 Habits of Highly Effective People*, using his time management quadrant. After grinding through every single task that they have over the course of the day, the only thing that was both urgent and important was prime pitching time (i.e., time devoted strictly to new client prospecting) because this is what more directly creates revenues and everything else could be scheduled elsewhere. Everything else is optional or comes later.

	Urgent	Not urgent
Important	1	2
Not Important	3	4

Fear of rejection is a big reason why some people don't get into sales. They're very apprehensive about what the reaction might be when reaching out to people they don't know or who may not necessarily know about their products or see value in their products. You have to get used to being told no and be able to see prospecting as a numbers game—something that's also solvable by people getting to understand what your product does.

You can overcome fear of rejection through reframing. For example, people will want to buy the product I sell once they fully understand it.

Another reframing technique is to see rejection as an opportunity to learn and improve so you celebrate each rejection as a step closer to a yes.

There's the *lack of preparation*. People may struggle with prospecting if they're not prepared. To overcome this challenge, research prospects so you can understand their needs and pain points and be able to create a personalized approach. For example, you can prepare an impact statement that creates intrigue or establishes common ground.

If you're prospecting someone, you want them to think it's the only call, or one of the few calls, you're making today, because there's a unique piece of information that justifies the call and doesn't make the prospect feel mass-targeted. This unique point could either be something that you have in common, such as a person you both know or a macro trend, like a regulatory change, that justifies the call in the mind of the prospect.

In terms of measuring the success or effectiveness of fanatical prospecting in creating leads and driving sales, the number-1 metric is the *number of qualified leads* or *sales opportunities* generated through the prospecting effort. This measures the number of leads generated compared to how many are engaged and how many can be advanced to higher levels in the sales process.

At the other end are *conversion rates*. There are different milestones, as we mentioned when we discussed KPIs. Conversion rates would be at the end of the process, measuring the percentage of leads that converted into customers. This would be the ultimate indicator of the quality of leads generated during the sales process. *Sales revenue generated* measures total revenue generated for the sales made through the prospecting efforts. This is an important metric since it directly impacts the company's bottom line for return on investment. Also, there's the *average sales cycle length*. This measures the average time it takes for a lead to become a customer.

Setting Up Sales Opportunities

There are several effective channels or methods for setting up sales opportunities. In the years before the pandemic, the narrative being pushed from certain quarters, especially platforms like LinkedIn, was that cold-calling was dead. Presumably, this was because it wasn't to LinkedIn's advantage for cold-calling to continue as the primary way to set up pitch opportunities—instead, that platform was trying to get salespeople to pay for LinkedIn Navigator and set up pitch opportunities prospecting with LinkedIn. That was a part of their sales strategy, and people who didn't like the idea of cold-calling, or had tried it and hadn't had success with it, readily brought into LinkedIn's pitch.

Cold-Calling

Unequivocally, *cold-calling* is the most efficient way to get prospects on the line and a direct way to begin the sales process. This is especially true if the purpose of the call is to set up an appointment, which might require building enough value during that phone call to motivate that decision-maker to agree to a face-to-face meeting shortly thereafter. This can work well if one accepts that their product might have a long sales cycle. Cold-calling is also the most efficient way if the purpose of the call is to close the deal then and there.

Cold-calling was revolutionary when it started being used in the insurance industry in the early twentieth century. As described earlier, insurance industry leaders, armed with sales teams, just started calling everyone up and down every organization, selling them insurance in a highly efficient way, because they no longer had to knock on doors.

I believe that cold-calling is still a robust approach today, but it is something that companies perhaps don't now favor as much as other methods. Telecom companies have made cold-calling more difficult, with technology that sometimes profiles outreach calls negatively, electronically labeling phone lines that make a lot of calls as "spam" or "sales." This, combined with call number transparency through call display, means that sales organizations have to be more and more creative to ensure that their salespeople can dial and get the right people on the phone without technology interfering with or blocking their efforts.

We'll cover ZoomInfo (which is different than Zoom Video Conferencing) later on. But it's a great way to get cell phone numbers and direct lines to customers, and people who are highly skilled at cold-calling are going to turn a cold call into a warm call very quickly by finding common ground so the prospect engages with the call, even if it interrupts whatever they're doing.

Email Prospecting

In addition to cold-calling, *email prospecting* is something I've gradually gained experience with over the last decade. In particular, through the pandemic and thereafter, reps sending targeted emails has been an important method of reaching customers and setting sales appointments to do a sales pitch, either by phone or Zoom VC.

Email prospecting is important, but it is something that requires greater finesse as the volume of emails that prospects are getting increases overall, other "noise" clamoring for their attention increases, and more messages are filtered out as spam. Email prospecting was possibly easier to do for a period following the pandemic, but now it's getting increasingly challenging. As a result, you have to get better at using it and make adjustments as necessary.

LinkedIn Outreach

LinkedIn Outreach is a lot like email prospecting, but within communities that are more fixed and better organized through the platform. It involves sending targeted messages to potential customers with an introduction, information, and call to action, often to set up a meeting or demo. That is also the aim of email prospecting, but the key difference is that the depth and credibility of one's existing LinkedIn community, including common connections with the prospect, will often affect the success rate.

For both strategies, I can have one person sitting on my left generating two percent responses to their emails and their LinkedIn, so they don't even have time to manage the volume that they would need to create enough pitch opportunities to predictably close deals through this strategy. And I can have someone sitting on my right who can generate 20 percent returns on those emails, if they put in the time, and send strategic follow-up emails and/or calls shortly after the initial email. It has to do with the content of the messaging and the follow-up choices of engagement that make it work for one person, but fail for another.

Referrals and Content Marketing

This approach has evolved, and over time, my teams increasingly utilized this to their advantage. *Referral prospecting* is about asking existing customers or business partners for referrals to new customers who may be interested in their product or service. When you deliver a great product or service, asking "Who else do you know that would benefit from this" can be a great question. This is only so, however, if it doesn't create additional competition at the expense of your clients so they avoid disclosing strong leads. Being sensitive to that is important, and if scarcity or urgency was used to book the client, you need to make sure that approach does not contradict this and/or the conditions that motivated the client to have committed.

Content marketing involves creating valuable content, such as blog posts or white papers or case studies, to attract potential customers and motivate them to contact the company for more information or to set up a meeting or demo.

Trade Shows

Trade shows are the traditional way a lot of people have used to create sales leads. They set up a booth and try to turn handshakes into business conversations and collect business cards in a fishbowl. The risk of that type of event is that you're often meeting with other sellers, not buyers, and non-decision-makers. You spend a lot of time trying to collect business cards that you might take back to the office to give to your sales teams to turn into prospects.

In the last two or three decades, the trade show strategy has, arguably, become less and less effective in helping companies generate new customers. When participating companies struggle to find ROI evidence from attendance at their previous trade shows and want to pull out, a common threat by some trade show organizers is to suggest that this will create a stigma of financial vulnerability for those firms, causing some firms to begrudgingly continue year after year.

Events that set up one-on-one meetings between buyers and sellers in a highly qualified way are even rarer. Such events, which I've worked on personally for many years, focus on the end of the sales process that every company is trying to achieve rather than the engine that creates leads, which the trade show is usually about. So it's important to choose the type of event according to where more advanced sales opportunities can be generated.

4 Steps in Sales Prospecting

Research the prospect
Understand structure of the organization, their industry, and recent news.

Identify decision-makers
Do organizational mapping, join networking groups and try to get a referral.

Understand Priorities
Decipher what matters to potential customers and provide solutions to end goals.

Engage with prospects
Create pitch opportunities through a variety of mediums such as phone, email, Linkedin and events.

Improving Closing Ratios

A vital step in improving closing ratios is personalizing and tailoring your outreach efforts for different channels and target audiences. The first thing is to establish your target audience. In starting any outreach, it's important to have a clear understanding of the target audience, including their demographics, interest, pain points, and other relevant information to customize messaging. Once you have a clear understanding of your target audience, you can *customize your messaging* to resonate with their needs and interests.

Use the right tone. The tone of your message can make a big difference in the perceptions of your target audience. Some industries, such as manufacturing or industrial, might respond better to more casual language, whereas a more formal tone might be more appropriate for legal or investment industries. Different channels require different approaches.

LinkedIn would be a more professional platform, so that messaging should be more formal and professional, whereas social media platforms like Instagram and X (formerly Twitter) may require a more casual or conversational tone. As you go from one medium to another, it's important to test different things, maybe even A/ B testing, to see what works best. There are many best practices or tips for crafting compelling messages and engaging with potential clients through these channels.

A *personalized message* is important when sending an email or on a phone call. This can include using the receptionist's name on a call or referencing the recipient's interests or recent activity in an email in the subject line or opening sentence—many of such techniques can be used that have a massive impact on open rates and gaining people's attention. By citing something specific about their business and industry, you show that you've done your research.

Keep it short and sweet. People are busy and don't have time to read long messages or listen to long pitches, unless already engaged. Keep the messages concise, to the point, and highlight key benefits of the product or service and how they can help the recipient. This is tricky because when it comes to email messages that are going to leave them wanting more and cause people to make further inquiries, short and sweet is really the key. That's an art form: a pitch that's optimized over time and is the right length accomplishes the most. That's trainable and teachable.

Use a conversational tone. Avoid using jargon or technical language, which can be confusing to potential clients. I would add another criterion—*provide value.* Instead of focusing on the product or service, show potential clients where there's value—what's in it for them? Maybe that's industry highlights, news, or other useful information that can help establish you as a thought leader or build trust with prospective clients.

Don't be afraid to *follow up* with potential clients after the initial message. I've been tracking this, and I often find that more people reply to follow-up emails than the original message. With the email that comes after the first follow-up or second message that you send, the open rate is sometimes higher. From one hundred emails, you might get two people responding to your first message, and ten people responding to your second message, then with the third follow-up, you might get another three. You know what your response rate is if fifteen pitch opportunities can be created from one hundred emails (plus follow-ups). Or are you only creating five for every hundred emails? There is a big difference in output if you are generating 15 percent prospect engagement versus 5 percent rate.

Then, sometimes, in addition to sending a follow-up by email, if someone isn't answering, pick up the phone and just say, "Hey, I sent you a few emails. Would you like to talk about this or not?" Often, people will respond, "I've seen your emails. I've been wanting to reach out, but I'm just busy. Yeah, let's set a time." Often, it's the follow-up by phone to the email that makes the difference. Perhaps this can get someone to an 18 percent response on their email campaigns. So it really is a one-two-three "punch combination"—a process that includes an initial email, one or two follow-up emails twenty-four to forty-eight hours later, plus a follow-up phone call.

Overcoming Channel Challenges

You will encounter several specific challenges or barriers when using certain channels for setting up sales opportunities. In cold-calling, traditionally, the biggest challenge was getting through to the decision-maker because companies would have a front door into their phone line, and it would be very difficult to speak to anyone without talking to a gatekeeper. In those instances, there was also a backdoor automated number. And salespeople had ways of being able to get people's direct lines.

To overcome this challenge and successfully get through to the decision-maker requires a lot of research to find out who the decision-maker is, and having a very tight process for what to say and what not to say—not to the decision-maker but to the gatekeeper who's there to block people who are time wasters.

Now, with mobile phones published through databases, like ZoomInfo, prospecting a lot of people just means dialing a lot of cell phones. As a result, in 2024, it may be easier to get past the gatekeeper than in 2004. An all-fronts approach to calling the gatekeeper, calling the cell phone, and calling the direct line will often double and triple people's ability to create pitch opportunities through calling.

Other variables have to do with calling at different times during the day or week, when the gatekeeper may be less likely to answer the phone. As a strategy, many salespeople will start calling executives fifteen minutes before 8:00 am, local time, before their personal assistants start their day, and repeat this approach when dialing subsequent time zones. Then there are trends such as in investments: after the markets close may be a better time to reach a decision-maker.

Prospecting Using Database Tools

In this day and age, ZoomInfo and LinkedIn play similar roles but offer different results. Both provide vast amounts of information about potential customers. You can use them to sort by content, information, company size, industry, revenue, etc. They offer the ability to slice and dice information in myriad ways to create lead lists that are easy to manage.

This enables you to save time in creating lead lists that are quite curated. For example, you not only have many numbers for mobile phone numbers and direct lines, but you can also make that database more targeted by taking a person's title and matching a hundred other people who have a similar title in a similar industry and other characteristics in common.

Prospecting using database tools, such as ZoomInfo or LinkedIn, centers on using the software to identify potential customers who fit the ideal customer profile. You can search companies based on industry, revenue, location, and other criteria to find the best prospects for the business for lead generation. Once you've identified potential customers, you can use these databases to find contact information for decision-makers and influencers within those companies, allowing you to reach out to them directly and start building a relationship.

The sales intelligence that these databases offer can provide valuable insights into potential customers, such as recent news about their company, relevant events, their financial performance, and market trends in their sector. Such information can help tailor a sales approach to better resonate with prospects.

Before you can fully leverage the features and capabilities of ZoomInfo or LinkedIn to identify and qualify the potential prospect, you need to create your ideal customer profile. Once you understand that profile, you can determine factors such as the industry, company, size, location, and job titles that are most likely to lead to successful sales. You may have to dig a little bit to be able to shake the tree and find the best prospects.

Once you identify potential prospects, review their information in the database. Check indicators like their job history, company size, and responsibilities to see whether they're a good fit for your products or services. This is great information to have at your fingertips to more easily begin the sales process through outreach. These database tools have sales intelligence that embodies this approach.

There are many other features, and I believe they will only get better. The challenge is that the better that these database tools become, the more aware people also become—so when they get an email, they may not pay attention to it as readily. If an unknown number comes up on someone's iPhone, often people will not answer it and wait for a message or a text to see who it is. So it's a bit of cat and mouse with advancements in technology and sophisticated industry tools.

When I started in sales almost twenty-five years ago, we were using Hoovers, a database tool later acquired by Dun & Bradstreet. This was pre-Google. Many of these database tools were strange compared to today and had a lot of unreliable information. But they did provide a platform for people to reach out. As I mentioned in an earlier chapter, people would prospect by using magazines and just calling up the advertisers. This is not as primitive as finding leads in the phone book and indiscriminately calling everyone, but it does highlight how far we've come in a quarter century.

Now you can use things such as a company's social media presence to find leads. Companies that communicate on these platforms engage with potential vendors and often announce news and events. You can search for companies that have been in the news, have upcoming events, are making announcements, or have new product launches.

Limitations of Database Tools

There can be limitations and drawbacks when using database tools. *Incomplete or inaccurate data* is one. Sometimes the end of the database might be incomplete or inaccurate, which can limit the effectiveness of the search. It's important to use multiple sources to verify the data, so updating the database regularly is always an issue. If you rely too heavily on the information in the database, that can raise issues.

When you go into a sales call and say, "I know your revenue is twenty-five million dollars," and they say, "No, it's two hundred fifty million dollars," if you don't have a skillful rescue strategy to re-engage the prospect and re-establish credibility, you're done—you've lost, and the call will be over.

Another issue with some database tools is *limited search options*. Some database tools may offer search options that make it difficult to find the exact data that you're looking for. For example, it's pretty straightforward to use LinkedIn to find CEOs or presidents of pharmaceutical companies. But if you want to know which companies sell to pharmaceutical companies, it's much harder to use their search features to find that information.

Cost is another potential limitation. I look at how ZoomInfo protects their information and makes it available to one user at a time. This is protected by IP address, so if you log in and out too often from different IP addresses, they will shut you down. If you log into the software with the same IP address in New York and within five hours log in with the same IP address in London, they're going to shut you down because they know there's no way that you've been able to get across the ocean that fast. In the absence of hypersonic flights or the Concorde, that will be a red flag, and your ZoomInfo account will be shut down. So every ZoomInfo user needs their own account. They're expensive, because they know their value is high, and they diligently protect the use of their information. It's very hard for companies to share licenses or cut corners by streamlining. You really need a license for every user. That's their business model.

To commit to that type of technology is a huge cost, and while LinkedIn Premium has a more affordable monthly rate, it provides marginal extra value compared to the free LinkedIn for integration with other tools.

The Evolution of Database Tools

The pandemic allowed salespeople to adapt to an environment where people didn't work in the office, which, in turn, benefited ZoomInfo. Some of the traditional methods to create a pitch opportunity, such as calling someone in the office weren't possible during the lockdowns, but because ZoomInfo tracks a lot of mobile phones, being able to speak with people by using that tool was a lifesaver.

But things have shifted quite a bit over the years, and other database tools are available. For instance, in investments, tools such as Preqin and PitchBook help people identify money managers and others in the investment community to pitch to. If I were to go back twenty-five years, not only was there Hoovers, which I've mentioned, but also Ask Jeeves, which was later rebranded Ask.com. That was a search engine arguably more popular than Google at the time. There was also Thomasnet.com, which has been evolving for years in manufacturing—people have relied on it to help find efficiencies through their research efforts.

Things have really evolved. Over the course of my career, call display has become something that's used much more frequently. Back in the day, people had fewer mobile phones—it was hard to get their mobile phone numbers. People would have to prospect by calling the office, and an art that people prospecting by phone had to learn to get through gatekeepers has now been somewhat lost. It's perhaps analogous to hunters or trappers who can go out and live on their own in the woods without a supermarket—in some ways, that's what raw salespeople have had to do. They have a unique skill set—the ability to get through to the right people.

All these techniques in some ways have been rendered moot by cell phones. It's been a bit of cat and mouse over the last twenty-five years or so, with call display technology offering more and more transparency around phone calls. But there's always an adaptation.

In some ways, I would say that ZoomInfo, leading up to the pandemic, became a tool that allowed people to get through at a similar level of frequency that they might have previously, by giving people access to mobile phones more frequently. But I wouldn't say it was necessarily any more than that. It's probably "even Steven" when it comes to the number of pitch opportunities that it's created, with the exception being during the pandemic.

Now that we are past the pandemic, we're in a world where most executives know about ZoomInfo, and to a large degree, it's come full circle. As mentioned earlier, a lot of people will not answer their mobile phone if it's not in their directory or they don't know the number or linked to a name in their phone contacts. So more and more, the lost art of getting through gatekeepers has become important again, and it's a skill set that many younger salespeople have lost because they never had to do previously at any point in their career.

What this shows is how adapting to different business environments, which we have talked about elsewhere in the book, has also been affected by how we reach prospects to create pitch opportunities and how technology has helped but at the same time hindered the ability to do so.

CHAPTER 8

Working Smart

A strong sales performance is made up of three key factors: 1) working hard, 2) working smart, and 3) maintaining a strong mental attitude. If we master and optimize all those, sales performance can be predictable. We want to ensure that we consistently apply the right mindset to a high volume of cleverly executed opportunities.

"Working smart," within the context of sales teams, involves using resources, state-of-the-art sales processes, effective time management, and sensible adjustments along the way. It is different than working hard in terms of not just putting in more hours of effort, but using resources effectively to achieve desired outcomes—both in the short term and the long term.

For example, Cisco prioritizes working smart by having its sales teams leverage its vast portfolio, industry expertise, and partner ecosystems to provide comprehensive solutions that meet customer needs and create extra revenue.

To prioritize tasks and responsibilities to ensure that you and your sales team are working smartly and efficiently, I recommend the following steps:

1. Identify the most important tasks.
2. Set realistic goals.
3. Use data analytics.
4. Focus on high-value activities.
5. Delegate.
6. Use effective communication and state-of-the-art processes.

Delegating tasks is one way to optimize productivity and achieve better results without burnout. Too often, sales organizations try to make their salespeople responsible for everything in their repertoire. That tends to mean that salespeople who learn to close, which is probably the hardest task in an organization when it comes to revenue, often find themselves doing tasks that other people could do. I think smarter organizations are those that institutionalize a variety of tasks and provide time-saving measures to help their best people do only what they do best and ensure there's infrastructure to absorb the other tasks.

To help circumvent burnout, in addition to what we've discussed previously, set goals and prioritize tasks, delegate, and use time management to work for a set period, and then take a break to avoid burnout while maintaining productivity. It's important to help people take care of their physical and mental health by urging them to eat nutritious food, exercise regularly, sleep well, and take breaks throughout the day.

Encouraging a Culture of Working Smart

Sales organizations can take various measures to encourage a culture of working smart within a sales team. These include the following:

- ❖ Setting clear expectations at the start
- ❖ Emphasizing quality over quantity
- ❖ Using data to inform decisions and identify areas for improvement
- ❖ Fostering a culture of collaboration
- ❖ Providing incentives to encourage people to work smart

Tools for Working Smart

In the information era, sales teams must leverage technology and automation to work smart. Several tools and technologies can help streamline processes and improve productivity within a sales organization.

To start, again I would recommend *customer relationship management (CRM) software*. It helps sales teams manage their customer interactions, track sales progress, provide valuable insights into customer behavior, and shows how to approach each customer. The software also provides KPIs that allow sales reps and management to make adjustments to optimize their work decisions.

Sales-enabling platforms are used to help automate the sales process, providing sales teams with the right information, content, and tools at the right time. These will help make sales content more effective, while providing insights into customer engagement. *Marketing automation software* can help sales teams automate their marketing campaigns, including email campaigns, social media marketing, and lead tracking. This saves time and improves marketing initiatives.

Sales analytics tools can help sales teams analyze their sales data to identify trends and opportunities for improvement and facilitate data-driven decisions based on their overall performance.

Virtual meeting software such as Zoom VC or Microsoft Teams or Google Meet can help teams connect with customers and colleagues remotely, reducing travel costs while allowing effective communication and collaboration.

Aligning Sales Approach with Product Positioning

It's vital to align the sales approach with the positioning of the product you're selling. In some ways, this leads into what makes the product scarce or rare or valuable. As I noted before, people tend to want things that they can't have. How do you create that phenomenon and build that desire organically from strategies applied when pitching the product?

Positioning needs to be consistently spread throughout the pitch and be present in a congruent way in the beginning, the middle, and the end. A sense of urgency needs to be created through product positioning to yield value by driving revenue sooner rather than later.

Aligning the sales approach with the positioning establishes a strong connection between the product or service and the customer's needs, along with their reasons for buying. This leads to increased interest and higher sales success.

The following tips will help get the sales approach in alignment with your product positioning:

- ❖ Use storytelling to explain product positioning.
- ❖ Understand the target audience.
- ❖ Use the right language and tone.
- ❖ Demonstrate value.
- ❖ Provide social proof.
- ❖ Offer personalized solutions.

Negotiation Strategy Leveraging Product Exclusivity and Scarcity

There are various strategies you can use to leverage product exclusivity and scarcity as negotiation tactics to drive sales.

Offering exclusive access to products or services creates a sense of urgency and demand among customers, as mentioned earlier in the book. This is done very well by luxury brands who create limited editions of their products, creating a sense of exclusivity and scarcity. This broadens demand through the psychological trait of people wanting things that they can't have or valuing things that are exclusive and rare.

Creating a sense of scarcity around a product or service can help drive sales. Like some other strong brands, Chanel does this quite well with many of its products, particularly their classic purses in an ongoing way, by releasing limited quantities of their products at a time or getting people to pre-order, creating a continuous desire for their products instead of ramping up their manufacturing.

That's a very common approach—airlines do this by limiting seats on airplanes, forcing people to book ahead or risk losing their seats or paying more for them. The strategy is used for just about every product or service out there.

Limited-time offers of a product can also drive sales. They can help create a sense of urgency or scarcity. Any sale motivates people to buy because it contains an incentive. A discount is a reason to buy today because it's always for only a limited time and will invariably expire soon. Most products and services dabble with campaigns designed to provide compelling incentives to "Buy now!" to drive sales because such incentives are temporary and expire at a given point in time.

Offering early access to a product or service creates a sense of scarcity similar to a sale. What is different is that not everyone has the same privilege or access to the product early since perhaps only a certain class of customers can pre-order or get ahead of a normal product release to the general public.

The following are conditions or factors your sales teams should consider when utilizing exclusivity and scarcity in negotiation: Sales teams should evaluate *market demand* for the product or service they're offering. If the demand is high, exclusivity and scarcity can be more effective in driving sales. However, if demand is low, other strategies might be needed to make those products unique for certain markets, to give the sales teams an advantage. That could take the form of a change in price or service or other benefits that could be offered on a limited-time basis to drive sales and to give people good reasons to buy the products.

Sales teams should evaluate the level of *competition* in the market. If many competitors are offering similar products and services, can exclusivity create a competitive advantage and also drive sales? If there are only a few competitors, or if there are a lot of competitors, these strategies may be effective or not.

So, going back to my previous point, consideration needs to be given about how to give people good reasons to buy your product over others that are in the market.

Customer loyalty should also be taken into account. If customers are loyal, or they really have an interest in the brand, demand will be a lot stickier.

The *pricing* of a product or service can be increased when it's high quality. If it is above the typical market price, you might want to reduce pricing in some cases to give people reasons to buy it over others. These are just tweaks that could be made to the overall strategy, depending on where your product sits at any given time. But urgency needs to be the driving force or the byproduct of those adjustments, because all sales are measured on a continuum of time. Sales need to accelerate the amount of products sold and revenue generated over time.

Risks Associated with Using an Exclusivity or Scarcity Approach

An exclusivity or scarcity strategy carries several potential challenges or risks. These include the following:

The Perception of Dishonesty

When using this approach, salespeople must avoid the following traps: (a) making up stories, (b) being disorganized with their messages, (c) contradicting themselves, or (d) losing credibility. You don't want to damage a brand's reputation or customer loyalty by creating scarcity in a clumsy or dishonest way. To mitigate the risk, teams should be transparent about limited availability, and provide solid reasoning for exclusivity.

Losing Trust

If the customer feels the sales team is only interested in making a sale, that leads to a breakdown of trust. To mitigate this, the sales team should focus on building relationships, understanding their customers' needs, offering solutions that meet their requirements, including telling customers when a product isn't good for them, or advising them not to take a particular course of action, or explaining why conditions aren't right for a purchase. A top salesperson must always have a higher level of purpose beyond making more sales.

Negative Impact on Long-Term Sales

If you rely too heavily on exclusivity to drive sales, it may affect long-term sales. If your customers feel they were deceived, they may not return. To mitigate this, the sales team should focus on delivering high-quality products or services, making sure that if someone does buy early, they're servicing them well and laying the groundwork for future sales.

Overpromising

If customers come to believe that the product or service is not as exclusive or scarce as they were told, this creates disappointment and, very likely, no more purchases of anything you're selling.

Ethical Considerations

Sales teams must ensure that exclusivity or scarcity is ethical and in compliance with applicable regulations and laws. The tactics used should not be seen as unethical or tacky or indicative of a type of organization that someone wouldn't want to work with on principle.

Resistance and Indifference as Underlying Principles

Resistance is, to some degree, the opposite of the "Please, please, please, please buy my product, sir" approach. Resistance is more the attitude of "What is it about you that would allow me to justify letting you in the club or working with you?"

A lot of sales is perceived as being about persuasion, and as I've mentioned previously, sales is a big tent. Persuasion tends to be the negotiation tactic that children learn first. Some may also learn other techniques that can work on their parents, like indifference or aloofness, but many will continue to be mostly persuasive as teenagers and adults, invariably shaping how they also behave professionally.

I also talked about the lack of sales education for students in business schools, the lack of structure and how, after getting their first sales job post-graduation, they're inclined to use persuasion: "Please, please buy my product! Buy from me because you know my uncle." Or "Buy from me because I've called you every month for the last year and asked you about your family. Please. Come on, buy from me."

That's persuasion.

Resistance is creating the opposite effect. It's flipping the script. It's what banks and universities do: "Why should we give you the loan? Do you have any credit? How do we know you're going to pay us back? Okay, we'll think about it."

That's resistance.

Banks want your business, but they will decide on a higher interest rate if your credit is vulnerable. This is similar to being approved for admission into an exclusive university or club. Resistance is really the opposite of persuasion. It's a different flavor that contradicts how many people think about sales. It's really dependent on indifference as a method of bolstering credibility. After all, if one really is the prize, they shouldn't care whether someone buys or not since someone else will.

I could say, "If you're going to do this, you need to do it today." That could feel like pressure; indifference takes the edge off of pressure. "If we're going to do this, we're going to need to do it today, but if you can't, that's okay too."

Resistance and indifference work together to create a very different sales beast than the typical sales animal whose nature is defined by pressure to buy.

Practical techniques or tactics to leverage resistance and indifference are those that start with the question "Who is the prize?" That establishes a level of scarcity as part of the narrative about the product. The goal is to engender the understanding that not everyone is going to be approved—not everyone is worthy of the product, and there's a lot more that we need to know to be able to decide whether we can work together.

It's a simultaneous positioning that needs to be stated at the beginning. As Oren Klaff wrote about in *Pitch Anything*, it is winning the frame in the moment, establishing who is the prize and making sure that every element of the process follows that narrative consistently.

It's important not to lose credibility by contradicting yourself throughout the process and breaking the established frame. The question is, "Who wants who more?" That's sometimes a difficult thing to do for salespeople because their natural inclination is to abandon that frame when prospects decline and perhaps say, "No, no, you should do this…" as opposed to being indifferent if someone says no and saying, "Okay, fine, it doesn't look like we're going to do business together. But why did you want to do this in the first place?"

Re-engage in an unpersuasive way that doesn't contradict the frame.

Salespeople should aim to strike a balance between utilizing these alpha principles and maintaining genuine rapport and trust with potential clients. Here are some techniques that can help accomplish this:

- ❖ **Be authentic**. Be honest and transparent about communication.
- ❖ **Listen actively**. Listen to potential clients' needs and concerns and respond in a way that demonstrates that you understand them.
- ❖ **Provide value**. Build the right amount of value to give people reason to prioritize your product or service.
- ❖ **Tailor your approach**. Customize your approach to the needs of the client.
- ❖ **Respect boundaries**. Don't push too hard or be too aggressive. Diplomacy is making a strong point without making an enemy, and that is an important attribute in being effective in delivering a sales strategy.
- ❖ **Follow up**. It shows that you value their time and input—and whether it's a yes or a no, being able to go back and check in can often yield future sales.

With regard to follow-up, one approach is to say, "Look, I just wanted to reconnect to have a postmortem since we're now closing your file. Sorry we weren't able to make it work. But out of curiosity, what happened?" Finding out that there was something that you weren't aware of and a solution that could lead to a sale, regardless of failure the first time, is only going to be discovered retrospectively through follow-up. And because potential customers sometimes only realize that they really want your product after experiencing the emotions associated with not being able to have it, completing the sale may require the courage to take it off the table before re-engaging (with credibility) to see if their desire to move forward has shifted because of an emotional reaction after the fact.

Strategic Time Management

Strategic and data-driven time management centers on optimizing your time to boost productivity and success. Steps in this process include these:

- ❖ Prioritize activities by analyzing data on leads, deals, and customer behavior.
- ❖ Identify bottlenecks.
- ❖ Track performance.
- ❖ Forecast revenue.

For best practices or tools in data-driven time management, I would again recommend CRM software. A good CRM is absolutely key to helping sales teams track and analyze data related to leads, opportunities, and customer interactions.

It's also important to *set goals and priorities*. Using data and insights, teams should set clear goals and priorities to help them focus their time on the most important things required to drive revenue growth.

Another best practice is to *analyze activity data*. Sales teams should track and analyze their activity data, such as number of calls made, emails sent, meetings held. This can help you identify which activities are most effective and which need improvement. This has been shifting back and forth since the pandemic in terms of calling, emailing, and LinkedIn prospecting.

For example, in our business during the pandemic, unless a sales rep had a prospect's mobile phone number, targeted messaging via email or LinkedIn was sometimes the only way to engage a prospect if they weren't in the office as much and mostly working from home. However, if the mobile phone number were available, the likelihood that someone would pick up the call was higher. Since the pandemic, the frequency of prospects engaging with email/LinkedIn prospecting seems to have declined, currently making cold-calling a much more important part of prospecting.

It's also beneficial to save sales teams' time by *automating routine tasks*. They can *use time-tracking software* to monitor how they're spending their time and see where they can be more efficient. This can help managers to identify which team members may need additional support and training or other resources, or delegate work that other people can do.

Also, *conduct regular performance reviews based on data-driven metrics* to identify areas of improvement and gather feedback for ongoing development.

Optimizing the Use of Communication Tools

Given the broad array of communications tools available, how can you strike a balance between utilizing different media, such as email, text, phone or video calls, or in-person meetings in your team's communication strategy?

A few factors come into play when answering this question. First of all, we want to rely on KPIs to make informed decisions around what's working, particularly when it comes to prospecting. So we want to understand, for example, how many emails it would take to set up a pitch opportunity and the efficiency of that process. We want to know how many leads are required to create a sufficient volume of pitch opportunities compared to applying a calling strategy.

Patterns can be analyzed by comparing the two, which would tell you whether someone should be putting more focus on an email strategy or a calling strategy.

As I mentioned previously, I've seen some reps who can set up appointments with 15 to 20 percent of their emails through a strategy that involves some follow-up exercises, but I've also seen others who are getting only 2 to 5 percent. If someone's not getting 10 percent for that level of activity, applying a calling strategy to their leads might be a better approach. When it comes to reps who are using the phone to prospect, I'd usually be looking to get through10 percent of the time, so every ten dials getting through to a decision-maker. If it's a lot less than that, adjustments need to be applied to that activity as well.

Then you can build in other means, such as text, that some salespeople are using to get attention. But some people may feel that's a little too intimate a method to reach someone cold.

When it comes to video calls, it's important to consider whether to use that avenue on the first call or on the second call, since such calls mostly need to be scheduled. Sometimes there are advantages for the first call for the rep to be a little bit anonymous and not allowing the prospect to pay attention to nonverbal cues. On a phone call, compared to Zoom VC or Microsoft Teams with the camera on, they are only hearing the voice of the rep describing, through tone, pace, and pauses, the essential information needed to decide whether to consider something further. By comparison, a video call might be more necessary on a second or third call to provide credibility and create the extra trust needed for someone to sign a contract.

Then, of course, there are *in-person meetings*. Many companies have a preconceived notion that if they're going to close a large deal of a significant size, they need a one-on-one meeting face-to-face, using the phone or email or both to set up a visit. Having the confidence to know when closing the sale by phone is just as effective as closing the deal in a boardroom and when there are diminishing returns is a strategic choice as well. It really depends on the nature of the sale.

There are some specific considerations or guidelines to follow when determining which communication tool to use in different situations. When measured, *the success rate in prospecting* would likely be the number-1 determinant, but in addition, customers sometimes have a particular preference. Taking that into account can be a factor. But maybe even more important than that, there's always going to be urgency in any sales call or reasons for people to buy. It's important to adjust to that urgency and highlight that urgency as justification for a phone call or a text message that requires immediate attention. Thus, real-time communication can be justified through points of urgency.

Another factor might be *the complexity of the communication.* Beyond a certain point, most salespeople are not going to want to write down things in an email. To do the most effective sales positioning, they're going to want to describe their value proposition and current situation, having an opportunity to evoke emotion in the prospect, sometimes by phone, sometimes by video call, and sometimes through an in-person meeting.

Additionally, *the relationship stage* is an important factor to gauge. When the sales relationship is fairly advanced, more informal approaches, such as text or WhatsApp, might be acceptable and more effective. That type of abbreviated informal communication can often be very efficient, and the type of message would also be a factor in this. What requires immediate action or confirmation may be best conveyed through a phone call or a text message.

Finally, *privacy and security* implications sometimes influence whether someone would use a phone call to convey some information, as opposed to putting something in writing or on WhatsApp that could be easily forwarded, etc.

CHAPTER 9

High-Probability Prospecting

Characteristics of Good Leads/Prospects

There are different ways of determining the key characteristics that make leads highly desirable or qualified. These can revolve around particular demographics or other factors, or we can play the numbers game.

Free social media platforms such as Facebook and Instagram are monetized by using customer data to help sellers get their products in front of highly qualified customers. Google does the same by using search to find high-probability customers and by leveraging its vast amount of user data and sophisticated algorithms. Clearbit, founded in 2015, was acquired by HubSpot in late 2023 and grew rapidly during this period by offering enrichment capabilities that help businesses both enhance and supplement their existing customer data and prioritize fresh leads based on various criteria. As such, salespeople using their solutions can focus on high-probability prospects while personalizing their outreach. The market for high-probability prospecting tools has become huge since this is also a top priority for those who run sales teams. Nevertheless, there are many ways of also narrowing down leads independently without necessarily having to rely on technology.

If someone's just going through the phone book and dialing name after name after name, a certain percentage of those leads, in theory, are going to close. If it's a B2C venture, there are ways to increase the probability of closing.

I once interviewed a woman who sold solar panels to consumers. The way her company narrowed leads down was by looking at consumers in states with more sunshine days in a year and locations where people had higher levels of disposable income. They basically targeted prospects by focusing on just those two factors. That's how they prioritize who to call, and that probably gives them a slightly higher percentage of closes.

But that's still fairly random. It's similar to calling people in the phone book. They just tried to narrow it down based on a few obvious characteristics. If we're in B2B sales, then it's about trying to narrow down leads by identifying what the key characteristics might be, and trying to call the highest probability ones first.

The first step is to look for prospects that fit with a product or service. A desirable lead or prospect is one with a genuine need for the product or service offered. Then align that with the target market and the pain points and the requirement to be effectively addressed by the solution being offered. That requires a certain amount of business analysis.

Second, *budget and resources* are sometimes going to matter. So, if you're selling something that's quite expensive, only a certain group of people or companies can actually afford it, based on the revenue they generate and the size of the company. It's important to figure out if there are ways of slicing and dicing this broad market into narrower strips that are going to give slightly higher closing percentages if you home in on those people first, and then also home in on the decision-making authority. Often, that comes down to either targeting that person or targeting the person who is the user, or both. Sometimes these are two different strategies.

The process where you pitch the person with the budget, often the president or CEO, could also be described as a top-down approach. You say, "I appreciate that you're not the user, or the technical person. But if your user supports this, because of the ROI that it generates, would you authorize the budget?" Other people might, in a bottom-up approach, find it easier to pitch the user of a product and hope that person will break down the barriers to push this up the ladder to the individual who actually has the budgetary authority to pay for it. These are two different approaches with different challenges.

Timing can play a role in lead qualification. Some people are actively addressing a need, so the problem your solution solves is actually already on their agenda as a part of a strategic plan. Other times, they have a problem, but either they haven't even identified it or they haven't set an agenda to fix it, or solving the problem isn't part of their strategic plan, or it's not on their list of priorities.

Sometimes, the key to making the sale comes down to finding ways of shuffling your product up the priority agenda by making it more important than other things that they intend to spend money on.

Evaluating long-term potential is important. Is there a chance for repeat business? Is it likely that this sale will be a feeder into other needs that you have products for? These are some of the factors that lead to prioritizing pitching one company over another, or one consumer over another.

In terms of a specific demographic or other factors to consider when evaluating the quality of a lead, some common attributes or characteristics tend to indicate a higher probability of conversion. Consider the following:

❖ Industry
❖ Company size
❖ Job title or roles
❖ Geographic location
❖ Revenue or budget
❖ Technology compatibility
❖ Pain points or challenges

Beyond demographic factors, look for specific behavioral or psychographic indicators in potential leads to assess their level of interest, engagement, or readiness to make a purchasing decision.

For example, *engagement with marketing content* is a huge flag. There are software solutions that allow people to send out marketing information to customers and see how they interact with the material: how often they go to it, how often they forward it to another person, what videos they're looking at, what pages they're reading, etc.

Also consider *how people respond to outreach*. If you send them an email saying you want to set up a conversation to discuss this, sometimes people will engage right away. Other times, they will ignore you and need to be pushed to engage. Sometimes, that indicates their lack of interest. Often, it's inconclusive until they either engage with your follow-up message, or you reach them on a call.

Sales signals such as searching relevant keywords, visiting industry forums, review sites, engaging in discussions—these are all things that can be used to understand the intense signals that may result in a purchase.

Consider *past purchase history* also. Sometimes you have a client who just loves to buy. I can think of one in particular. Every time we introduced a new product or service, this person would get satisfaction from buying it. They are more likely to purchase, based on how they behaved in the past.

Leads that actively provide *feedback* or detailed questions or seek clarification about the products or service are often more engaged or interested. This can demonstrate a willingness to explore and follow up. It doesn't always mean that they're more likely to buy, but it could be a strong indicator.

With regard to defining and creating ideal customer profiles (ICPs), I like the idea of looking at the characteristics of high-probability clients. I've seen many times how identifying and targeting good leads resulted in significant sales growth or revenue generation. It's important to be able to identify whether the lead is in a core category or a fringe category.

One example is investments, where a pattern was observed that first-time funds and money managers whose assets are under several hundred million dollars were unlikely to close because they would need income from those assets to afford an offer. That made them a much lower probability, and, if approved, we would only close perhaps one in twenty-five or one in forty compared to, under other circumstances, one in five or one in ten.

Another example comes from industries such as manufacturing or energy. Companies with less than $50 million in revenue would be lower probability because of cost, which would usually rule them out as well, or at least make prospecting them more of an exception.

Decision-making Process

To determine who the typical decision-makers involved in the sales process are, I would go back to what I've said previously—it really depends on whether you're focusing on the people who sign off on the budget or the people who are the users. A lot of companies in B2B sales decide who to target based on those two different approaches.

One is a top-down approach, where you would start with the CEO or the top person, and then be able to get anyone below the CEO who would weigh in on the decision. By making sure that the CEO is your prime point of contact and supports your proposition, those lower in the hierarchy may just fall into line. I think that is usually the most expeditious way to get sales done. If you can reach the CEOs, it's probably the preferred way.

With lower-level people, it sometimes takes much more effort to reach a CEO than it does to reach a VP, and you often need creative strategies to do so. So it's easy to drop down a level and take a no from someone who can't unilaterally say yes, but this trade-off is arguably not worth it.

It really depends on what companies feel they can achieve. A lot of companies accept a snail's-pace sales cycle, where they start their prospecting with a user or manager, and they trust that the manager is going to take it to their director and show them the benefits. Then the director is going to get behind it and take it to the VP. Then, maybe, it'll eventually get to the point where they'll all line up outside the CEO's door and say, "You have to pay for this." This would be considered a bottom-up approach. Maybe it will work out. But there are many points where things can go wrong through that process, causing a lot of frustration. It's a much longer sales cycle and, for obvious reasons, doing it that way can significantly increase the cost of sales.

To summarize, I would say: 1) identify the decision-maker as being the one who signs off on the budget; 2) recognize the influencers; and 3) recognize the users and come up with a plan that considers all three fully or, to some extent, recognize that the decision-maker is mandatory and the others are optional.

After all, finding an alpha decision-maker in a centralized decision-making process who is willing to act unilaterally is typically an easier sale to make, comparatively speaking. (I'll get into centralized or decentralized decision-making processes and the personalities of decision-makers later in this chapter).

You can use a variety of strategies or techniques to navigate complex decision-making structures within organizations to ensure you're targeting the right individuals and building relationships with key stakeholders. It depends on whether it's top-down or bottom-up, so it's important to do in-depth research to understand the dynamics of the organization.

❖ **Get the CEO's contact info**. If it's a top-down strategy and you're trying to expedite matters, get the

CEO's name and make a call. If you're doing bottom-up, you may want to research who the other decision-makers are.

❖ **Use organizational charts**. If you're doing a bottom-up approach, you've got to know where everyone is in the company hierarchy. That's not really necessary in the top-down approach.

❖ **Network within the organization**. You're going to have to network if you're doing bottom-up strategizing. Some people leverage existing relationships. That's what they need in order to push things up the ladder. This is usually not relevant in a top-down approach.

❖ **Engage with gatekeepers or not**. If building a relationship with the gatekeeper will cause them to let you know when the CEO is in and help you connect, that's a good strategy. If engaging with them means giving information that can be used against you, reducing the likelihood of you getting through, it would be counterproductive to be too visible with the gatekeeper.

Here's a few other points: *Provide value* at all levels. That's the bottom-up approach. *Seek consensus and alignment.* That's really a decentralized bottom-up approach with a split decision-maker and process that's decentralized.

Be persistent. This applies to just about everything. When we commit to a top-down approach, I would much rather have my staff wait several weeks and make multiple attempts to reach the decision-maker and not drop down a level to speak with a VP who has no authority to make a sales decision. I know the value of them waiting and getting the decision-maker on the phone. Presenting the pitch opportunity to that person is exponentially greater than dropping down a level or two and trying to fight to get it pushed up to the decision-maker.

Holding off on pitching to someone can be a strategic and tactical decision.

In a top-down decision-making process, there are often split decision-makers. Establishing what that decision-making process involves is a key part of any potential sale. Sometimes there's a decision-maker who will say, "Well, it's my decision." But when you ask the supplemental question, "What percentage of the decision is yours?" sometimes you find out it's 80 percent, but other times it's just 50 percent.

If it's 50 percent, I would apply a different strategy for closing the sale. If it's 80 percent, I would try to determine if the decision-maker can withstand the internal criticism of subordinates and push a deal through. I would ask questions like, "Okay, you say you want to do this, but what would you say if your team says no?" "Have there ever been times where your team has given you advice to not do something that turned out to be unhelpful to your business?"

Another approach might be to attempt to get persons with influence on the next call by saying, "Look, this isn't going to happen if John and Sheila aren't involved. Let's set up another call, go through it with them, and see if it works for them too. If not, let's forget about it, it's not going to happen if everyone doesn't agree." Be able to set up the next step to account for the split decision-making process.

Then there are the personalities of the decision-makers. Decisive decision-makers are more alpha and are often described as resolute, determined, firm, assertive, or proactive. They know what they want, they go for it, they're determined, and they have clarity about their decisions. That's the type of person that you can be confident is going to make decisions. It's easier to sell to that type of person than to indecisive decision-makers, who can be characterized as hesitant, tentative, uncertain, or wishy-washy. Such individuals like covering their tracks sometimes for political or self-preservation reasons and prefer other people to make the decisions. You just know they're going to be way more influenced by other people. It's harder to get commitment from them.

There are various challenges or obstacles when dealing with decision-makers. The key is to find ways to overcome these barriers and build trust and credibility with key individuals or decision-making teams. In the top-down approach, again, decision-makers are often protected by *gatekeepers* whose job is to filter out unsolicited sales calls or messages. Sales professionals need to develop strategies to effectively navigate around gatekeepers to reach decision-makers directly.

I remember in the early 2000s this top-executive with a Fortune 500 company whom I had to contact in Texas to make a sale. We considered him to be one of the hardest-to-reach persons we were targeting. The difference between making a sale or not came down to reaching him, and nobody else had been able to engage with him by phone. I had to go in and be really sweet with his assistant to have her give me inside information, such as when exactly he would be back in the office and how I could connect with him when he was out of the office by Blackberry, and that eventually got me talking to him and allowed me to make the sale.

There's the *resistance to change*. Decision-makers are used to doing things a certain way. So when you introduce a new product, a lot of the time they're going to say, "No, we don't need this." I went through this not long ago with a new hire, who was saying to me, "Look, I called them up, and they said they didn't need this."

I said, "Everyone is going to tell you that what they're doing is right. What you have to say is, 'Okay. Maybe we're not going to work together. But what are you going to do instead to improve your business? Have there ever been times when you would have wanted better results?'" A decision-maker who's resistant to change is only going to want to engage with a salesperson who believes in their product and challenges them, possibly even makes them feel foolish for not considering something differently (intelligently and tactfully, of course).

Such situations require salespeople to challenge their prospects, much like the sales methodology outlined in a 2011 book by Matthew Dixon and Brent Adamson called *The Challenger Sale*. Their key idea is that challengers take control of the sales conversation, pushing customers out of their comfort zones and encouraging them to reevaluate their needs and priorities.

There are competing priorities too. Decision-makers have a lot on their plate, and they're only going to allocate time where it's available. I get cold-called myself. I got a call from someone a while ago about insurance, and the guy wanted to set up a meeting with me. I asked him, "Is this about group insurance, or are you selling me personal insurance? What is this about?"

He said, "I want a meeting."

I said, "I'm not going to take a meeting unless I know what this is all about."

He said, "Okay, thank you." And he hung up the phone. I just wanted to know what it was about so I could rank it with all the other priorities I had to consider. That salesperson did not address that point particularly well and he will never know whether he lost a sale or not because he did not build enough preliminary value for me to want to know more and prioritize.

Many *constraints* to decision-making can be obstacles to making a sale. Some alleged decision-makers have a budget, some don't. Some have the authority to sign off. Others have to go to boards of directors. These are different situations. Questions about the process are going to help salespeople understand where they need to go to gain full support for a purchase.

This also applies to *complex decision-making processes*. Sometimes a decision-maker is only going to stick their neck out so far because they know that there are people who might chop it off.

Lack of trust can also be an issue. Decision-makers may be skeptical of sales professionals and their intentions. They might think that you just want to make a sale. That's why you gain credibility by saying, "Maybe this isn't something you should do. Look, I'm here to evaluate whether this is good for you and good for us."

Company Size

While company size is a factor in predetermining the potential of a lead to become a sale, it's less so than the decision-making process. All companies can set up complex or simple decision-making processes. With a traditional hierarchy, when there's a CEO and VPs and other people who have specific roles, decision-making is often centralized.

But sometimes public or private companies will have a layer of complexity that's deliberately created by the board of directors to allocate funds in a certain way that lets them maintain control. That might be less so when a CEO is also a founder of the company and controls most of the shares.

Company size doesn't always come into play. Very small companies may be good lead targets as well because they may be well-funded. You can't really slice and dice it solely according to size, but it is an indicator to be considered.

This also applies to sales cycles. In theory, a smaller company with a simplified decision-making process could have a shorter sales cycle than a larger company that has a more complex decision-making process.

But, again, other factors come into play. If a company has a lot of pain, and a CEO with discretionary budgeting authority to solve pain, and they want your product more than they want time to evaluate it, sales cycles can be very short.

There are many preconceived assumptions about a direct correlation between the size of a company and the simplicity or complexity of the sales process. I think that it's something to consider, but it has to be taken in context. So do your research without relying upon those preconceived notions. It's only one indicator.

If someone is researching a certain industry or trying to establish themselves in an area, they're going to see trends. Maybe someone is going to say, "It's not worth my time to pitch a company that's less than fifty million dollars on this particular product." Maybe above $50 million, your closing percentages might be one in five or one in ten, whereas if it's less than $5 million, maybe it's one in twenty-five or one in fifty.

So there are going to be correlations related to closing percentages that have to do with the size of a company. But, arguably, the personality of the CEO may be a more important factor. Similarly, it might be harder to pitch to a company where the board of directors has pitted a CEO and a CFO in an adversarial position to argue about spending decisions, which some companies do to create checks and balances. You're probably only going to know that once you're in there.

Pain or Need

Pain or need can amplify how much a company wants a product. This primes them to purchase if they can see that the product or service that you are selling alleviates that pain or need and, through analysis, allows them to predictably solve their problems. Identifying pain points is crucial to the sales process because it allows you to better understand prospective customers, and to gain insight into what motivates them.

It's important to build rapport and trust and understand what's going on. Prospects want people to listen to them and respond promptly. Customers who have been burned and misunderstood will need to develop trust in the salesperson's ability to offer solutions. By addressing their pain points, salespeople can more easily build customer confidence.

Identifying the pressing pain points also helps salespeople differentiate offerings from competitors by helping their prospects focus on information that they might not have considered. That process may lead the customer to conclude that an affirmative buying decision would be the responsible thing to do to alleviate their pain. This can help in generating value-driven sales.

Here are some strategies for uncovering pain:

❖ **Active listening**. Give your full attention to the prospect's words, tone, verbal cues, and nonverbal cues, depending on whether you are face-to-face or over the phone or on a Zoom video conference. The objective is to pick up the subtle details and emotions that can reveal deeper pain points.

❖ **Ask open-ended questions**. Rather than asking questions that allow yes-no answers, salespeople should ask open-ended questions to try to get as much flavor about the nature of the pain as possible, using questions that start with "Why," "What," "How," "Describe," or "What do you think about?" There are types of questions labeled "pain point questions" further described in Chapter 11 that can bring to the surface hidden pain, such as "What are your thoughts on there being potential customers everywhere who don't even know your company exists?"

❖ **Digging deeper**. A prospect can mention a surface-level need, and sales professionals can dig deeper. Chris Voss in *Never Split the Difference* has a great technique for doing this called mirroring, which is about just repeating the last three words that someone said, causing them to have the natural inclination to want to elaborate on what they just said.

❖ **Empathy and emotional connection**. An emotional connection with prospects can encourage them to open up and trust that they're going to be heard, if that's what's important to them, or that the other person is going to use the information constructively and with integrity, as opposed to against them.

❖ **Storytelling**. Sharing relevant anecdotes, success stories, or case studies can help prospects relate to their own challenges. For example, if I were to say, "My clients tell me this…," often they will reply, "We heard that too…"

❖ **Collaborative problem-solving**. A static presentation is not the best form of delivery, whereas deliberative communication is collaborative and about having discussions that are built on the input of all parties, and the ensuing deep analysis and deep dives into the subject matter are optimal.

❖ **Research and presentation**. For any sales conversation, salespeople can absolutely find more pain through preparation and by doing advance work on the prospect's industry, competitors, and common pain points.

ROI Analysis

ROI (return on investment) analysis refers to the evaluation of financial returns or benefits that a prospect expects to gain from investing in a particular product or solution.

Key metrics or factors that salespeople should consider include the following:

❖ Cost saving
❖ Revenue generation
❖ Time savings

- ❖ ROI period
- ❖ Productivity improvement
- ❖ Customer satisfaction
- ❖ Total cost of ownership

Salespeople will want to communicate the ROI of their products or services for several reasons. First, to *communicate the value proposition*. ROI helps sales professionals highlight how the product or service can directly impact the prospect's bottom line and provide a positive outcome. ROI can also provide *justification for investment*. Prospects often need to justify purchasing decisions to stakeholders or decision-makers within their organization by presenting clear ROI analysis.

Salespeople can provide necessary information or evidence to support the prospect's decision to invest in their offering. Additionally, ROI helps support *product differentiation*. In a competitive market, understanding and effectively communicating ROI can set salespeople apart from their competitors and can showcase the financial gains or cost savings that the product or service offers. They can also develop and demonstrate a unique value proposition to differentiate themselves from others.

Another benefit ROI analysis offers is *decision-making support*. This provides prospects with the information they need to make informed decisions that evaluate potential benefits and weigh them against the costs or investment required. It can also help in *building trust*. Demonstrating a deep grasp of their prospect's business and their financial goals through ROI analysis builds trust by showing that the sales professional has made the effort to understand how their offering can contribute to the prospect's success.

CHAPTER 10
Infusing Strong Mental Attitudes into Sales Culture

The Importance of Positivity

A positive attitude means having a mindset that is optimistic and constructive. It involves focusing on the positive aspects of a situation and looking for solutions rather than dwelling on problems and maintaining that mindset despite any challenges or setbacks.

A positive attitude can also include being supportive, encouraging, and compassionate toward yourself and others. It's about approaching life with positive energy and a mindset that can increase happiness, resilience, and success.

A negative attitude means having a mindset or outlook that is pessimistic, cynical, or unconstructive. It involves focusing on the negative aspects of a situation, constantly complaining or criticizing, and expecting the worst outcome. A negative attitude can also include being dismissive and judgmental and unsupportive toward yourself and others. Approaching life with negative energy and mindset can increase dissatisfaction, block change, and hinder personal growth.

There's a very strong correlation between attitude and success in sales, and many companies recognize this correlation.

Salesforce is renowned for its emphasis on positive mental attitudes and strong sales culture, often referred to as "Ohana" by CEO Marc Benioff, which is the Hawaiian idea of family bonds that encourage people to be responsible for each other. The company promotes growth mindset and provides extensive training and development opportunities for its sales teams. Salesforce also fosters a supportive and collaborative environment, encouraging its salespeople to learn from each other and continuously improve.

HubSpot is a company that also puts a strong emphasis on mindset and provides resources and training to help its sales teams develop a strong mental attitude. Similarly, Google has a unique sales culture that values creativity, innovation, and a growth mindset. IBM has a long-standing reputation for its sales culture and the mental attitude of its sales people.

I've done a lot of interviews in my time. I previously mentioned that I've interviewed over two thousand candidates in helping to build a global sales workforce in different locations around the world. During many of those interviews I've asked many candidates directly, "Are you a positive person?" and I haven't met a lot of people who would describe themselves as negative. I've met a few realists and some cynics, but people's perception of themselves (at least in an interview situation) is fundamentally positive. It's very difficult for people to see themselves as negative because it is not considered a desirable attribute.

However, a lot of people misunderstand what being a positive person means. Sometimes I'll ask the question a little differently: "Would your friends describe you as a positive person?" This is an important aspect of sales. People will say that yes, their friends do. I say, "Why is that important to you?" And they may come back to me and say, "Well, people don't want to be around negative people. People are going to be better liked..." etc., etc. Every now and then someone will say, "Well, it's important to me, because if I'm positive, I'm going to be more successful," because some people attribute a relationship between attitude and success. Those are the ones where their commitment to positivity is usually a bit stickier because they have a deeper motive than someone who's just doing it for optics or superficial reasons.

Over time, I've realized that in sales it is particularly important that people have a strong mental attitude—ideally, a positive attitude—to achieve the most success. I've met a lot of people who, in the face of adversity, even if they consider themselves positive, blame external factors for their lack of success: "No one's picking up the phone," "Maybe our product isn't good enough," "Maybe the economy isn't good enough," "Maybe we're too expensive."

These examples represent a defeatist attitude toward common sales challenges that might thwart the motivation of salespeople to make adjustments and find solutions. I talked in an earlier chapter about tests meant to measure people's internal and external tendencies when it comes to taking responsibility for everything that affects them or blaming external factors. That really does come into play here.

Why is it important in sales? Because sales is a numbers game. Not everyone we approach is going to buy. It's similar to baseball—it's a game of failures. If you're batting 300 in the sport—which means you're failing to get a hit 70 percent of the time—you're doing pretty well.

In sales, who knows what "doing pretty well" really means? Being able to manage rejection and not have it paralyze or hurt you and stop you from what you're doing is very important. That takes resilience. It's an attitude that can usually protect against negativity. When people are playing a game of failures, unless they are prepared to accept that as part of the job, they can reduce their intensity or even give up, because it's not an easy road. There's a very strong correlation between attitude and success in sales.

However, a lot of businesses may be run by people who don't necessarily believe in positivity, don't take that approach themselves, and don't necessarily see this as being essential for their people. In such cases, it may be that they are leaving money on the table when it comes to doing things better or differently compared to an organization that focuses on people who are more resilient because they tend to maintain an optimistic attitude in good times and bad.

This also has to do with what is needed for salespeople to generate results. It takes multiple attempts. It takes small, isolated adjustments without necessarily being offended or bitter or shy or nervous about going back and adjusting your approach as needed and trying again. It's important to have a belief or expectation in good outcomes. You need to be able to see the light at the end of the tunnel in order to continue selling and perfecting and making adjustments along the way. If you don't see that the endgame is going to be something positive or relish in the uncertainty by trusting the process to deliver the envisioned outcome or another equally acceptable outcome, it becomes that much more difficult to maintain that attitude.

The ability to understand the endgame and be steadfast in pursuit of it is key. This is what creates the right pace and momentum for salespeople to make the adjustments they need at the right frequency to find success within the time they've allotted to prospect, find, and close clients. Many people will give up when the outcome is not predictable. But someone with a strong mental attitude will tend to be more resilient when it comes to persevering and finding a way through obstacles.

There's a great chapter in Napoleon Hill's *Think and Grow Rich*, I recall, about the oil driller who was drilling for oil and kept missing, missing, missing, missing, and then finally gave up. He sold all the equipment to someone, who just moved the location and angle of the drilling slightly and struck oil immediately after. A strong mental attitude is something that drives the follow-up that's often needed to find success after many multiple attempts or perceived failures.

For anyone wanting to create sustainable sales through a team, if they're hiring the right people or even when they're hiring people on the edge of the desired attitude with more risk, the goal should be to make sales results as predictable as possible. We've talked a lot about KPIs. We've talked about many different ways of helping reps forecast so they know that if they put in certain inputs, there will be corresponding outputs within a margin of error—and that's predictable. Structuring your sales process around people's attitudes and the need for their attitudes to maintain their hope is a key part of building the right sales team.

It's important to employ salespeople who can maintain a positive attitude amid adversity and failures. These are factors that, when applied at scale, are going to naturally create more success for those who are attentive to such traits.

How the Brain Is Wired

When our brain functions at higher frequency levels, we can more efficiently follow a process correctly and have the clarity to make elevated choices. Traditionally, neuroscience identifies four different types of brain waves that serve different purposes: delta, theta, alpha and beta. Delta waves operate at zero to four Hz (hertz, cycles per second) and are often associated with very deep sleep, while theta waves operate at four to eight Hz and are commonly observed during certain stages of lighter sleep, compared to delta, as well as during deep relaxation, meditation, and some forms of creativity, alpha waves occur in the frequency range of approximately eight to thirteen Hz. These waves are most commonly observed when an individual is in a relaxed and wakeful state with closed eyes. Beta waves are often associated with alertness, active thinking, and concentration and have a frequency ranging from twelve to thirty Hz and are generally observed when an individual is awake and engaged in cognitive tasks. Beta waves are often prominent in the frontal lobe of the brain. Many working people, including salespeople, tend to spend the majority of their working lives when awake in beta.

Gamma brain waves are a more recent discovery in the field of neuroscience and occur in the brain with a frequency range typically between twenty-five and one hundred Hz, but arguably up to two hundred Hz. These waves are associated with higher mental functions such as cognitive processing, memory formation, and problem-solving. Gamma waves are amongst the fastest brain waves and are often observed when the brain is highly active and engaged in tasks that require focused attention.

Gamma waves move from the back of the brain to the front of the brain up to forty times per second, touching all lobes of the brain, allowing an individual to bring together many different types of complex information into a single idea. The gamma brain state has been associated with higher levels of mastery and states of deep intuition and emotional intelligence that can be stimulated by experiencing positive emotions such as gratitude, appreciation, caring, and compassion. When someone is negative, they are unlikely to reach the higher level frequencies and brain functions that occur in gamma.

When someone is in a hopeful, positive place and can achieve gamma, a lot of information is recallable in a way that can be combined with other complex ideas, allowing enhanced perception and emotional intelligence. That helps people make better decisions in the moment.

HUMAN BRAIN WAVES

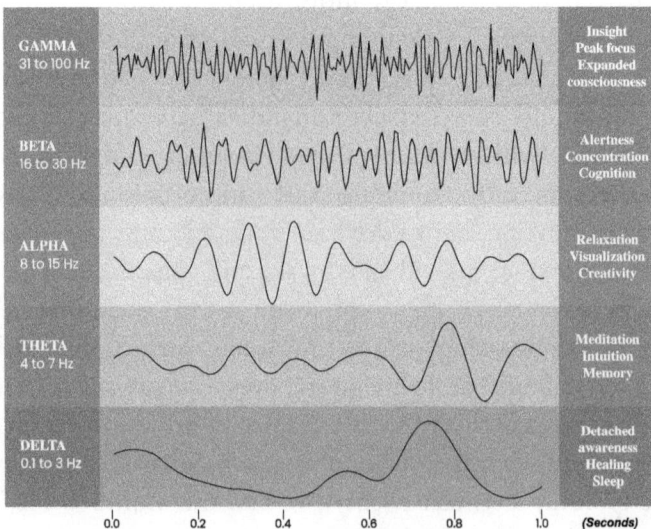

Other evidence suggests that mindset and the ability to maintain a strong, positive mental attitude helps people's brains perform in a way that allows them to be more effective. It's like an athlete warming up and visualizing before a match or a game, and going through a pre-competition routine to try to put them into an optimal space for enhanced performance.

Some people talk about tweaking your attitude or raising your consciousness before embarking upon any important activity, and I would say that best practice would also apply to sales.

There's been a lot of talk about emotional guidance systems and the use of feelings as a method of advanced decision-making. Whether it's Jose Silva, Napoleon Hill, or Dr. David Hawkings, or Abraham Hicks, or *The Secret* by Rhonda Byrne, all have talked about using emotions as feedback to determine whether one's mind is working positively or negatively. If you were to look at the bottom of the barrel of negative emotions, you would see desperation. That's what really causes people to have the most trouble moving forward. They're not in a good place. So, if someone who's desperate all of a sudden starts focusing on revenge, that's probably an improvement from desperation. Revenge isn't a great emotion, but it's at least better than desperation, because you care a little bit. Revenge isn't good, but if you're a little bit improved, maybe you're going to get angry, but you're not necessarily going to want to hurt people. So feeling anger instead of revenge improves your mental state to some extent.

Above anger is frustration. That's a milder form of discomfort, then there's pessimism, and then, eventually, hope. Hope is roughly the dividing point between positive and negative; when one is above hope, one can be happy.

Then there's joy, bliss, and enlightenment. Life is a matter of moments and decisions. Sales is a matter of moments and decisions. If you can devote part of your brain to always making sure you're above hope moment by moment, good things tend to happen in sales and in life. If we are falling below and spending a lot of our time in the negative emotions, we often get suboptimal experiences in those future moments—they're not quite how we want them to be.

EMOTIONS RANKED FROM POSITIVE TO NEGATIVE

JOY
PASSION
HAPPINESS
BELIEF
OPTIMISM
HOPE
COMMITMENT
BOREDOM
PESSIMISM
FRUSTRATION
OVERWHELMED
DISAPPOINTMENT
DOUBT
WORRY
BLAME
DISCOURAGEMENT
ANGER
REVENGE
HATE
JEALOUSY
UNWORTHINESS
DESPERATION

Believing in Positive Outcomes

Are luck and hardship bestowed randomly? Or is there a relationship between where we are and where we want to be? Will having our emotions charged positively or negatively respectively bridge or repel the gap between where we are and where we want to be? These are philosophical questions, but they arguably apply to sales. If we buy into the principle that we have more control over the future when we're able to charge our emotions positively and make good, thoughtful choices in the moment that allow our brainwaves to operate correctly, the application to sales can become even more relevant.

In addition to explaining the relationship between sales and attitude from neuroscience and self-help perspectives, we can also talk about the concept from a quantum physics perspective.

Quantum physics is a core branch of physics that describes the behavior of matter and energy at the smallest scales— typically at the level of atoms and subatomic particles. It is a highly successful and accurate framework for understanding the physical properties of the universe at the subatomic level, which arguably renders the Newtonian science that we learned in high school nearly obsolete because quantum physics is a wacky kind of science that is in many ways far more advanced. Many physicists will say that it is much closer to the truth than what most of us study in school. It is sometimes referred to as the science of possibilities. The argument is that at any particular moment, there are unlimited possibilities. Possibilities occur in waves, and moments occur in particles, and particles behave differently than waves.

Staying Positive in the Face of Adversity

Some scientists believe that quantum physics, when combined with ancient mysticism, can also be used to understand human consciousness. More specifically referred to as *quantum mysticism*, proponents argue that it is our belief in a particular outcome, from a plethora of other possible outcomes, that helps in the manifestation of any future moment. By understanding this phenomenon, and having people focus positively on outcomes that they believe in or want or expect, no matter how unlikely those might be, is often the key to creating those exceptional moments that defy reality.

For instance, the Hail Mary pass that wins the college football championship or the athlete who does something incredible in the moment. Such outcomes are remarkable and inspiring because there might be no odds to forecast such an unlikely occurrence. Arguably, it's the extreme belief by that athlete in such an unlikely outcome versus the doubt retained by an opponent as to whether such an unlikely outcome can be prevented, possibly complemented by the collective energy and belief (or doubt) of the communities observing the sporting event, that influences the possibility of one outcome or another manifesting in the moment.

Whether considering neuroscience, self-help, quantum physics, or quantum mysticism in relation to sales, we could go deeply into what this all represents. Either way, it is already broadly understood that more sales are created through a positive mindset and by believing that you're going to make sales than believing that you're not. This is why many sales organizations are all about getting their salespeople thinking positively. As evidence demonstrating the natural benefits of being more successful through mindset increases, no matter how best explained, business environments that encourage salespeople to feel this way will become more and more common.

That speaks to the question: is anything possible or not? Napoleon Hill said that whatever the mind can conceive, it can achieve. That is true, arguably, for people in all sectors of society, but particularly in sales, because, when I observe my best salespeople, they believe. They have a strong mental attitude. They set a goal, and they believe it's attainable. They expect the results to occur. They look for the signs that it's unfolding, and that tends to generate more revenue than people who believe the opposite, or are skeptical as to whether someone is going to buy their products.

Notwithstanding anyone's unique belief system, it is not illogical to believe salespeople will generate better results by expecting their customers will want to buy their products versus the opposite.

Using Flow to Drive Sales Performance

This leads into the topic of "flow," which is another way of looking at how to drive better performance.

In positive psychology, *flow state* is known colloquially as being "in the zone," the mental state in which a person performing some activity is fully immersed in a feeling of energized, focused engagement in the activity.

The Hungarian-American psychologist Mihaly Csikszentmihalyi first described the idea of flow. This state is often achieved by athletes in sports during competition or intense training, leading to new heights in performance. Musicians, artists, writers, and performers may enter a flow state when deeply engaged in their work, and the creative process can often be linked to flow.

Flow can also apply to individuals who experience this in their professional lives, particularly when working on tasks that are challenging and aligned with their skills. Creating an environment where salespeople can actually access a flow state—or achieve a level of flow in their minds—is something that I've experimented with for different sales teams. The goal is to try to create the momentum individually and collectively so the salespeople are totally focused on making good decisions.

I can speak for it myself: When I was at my best as a salesperson, I would be so focused on what I was doing to such an intense level that I was aware of nothing else. At such a time, I feel that I'm accessing information at a level beyond the hard drive of my brain. I'm tapping into collective energy to make decisions at a much higher level because I am in a positive state; I am in a state of flow. I can achieve that state of flow under certain conditions for short periods to create excellence in sales and to do things that I might not be able to normally do. So, there's an awful lot to be said for it.

When I played football, even though it was not my position, I used to practice kicking field goals for fun. Frequently, when selling by phone, I would imagine two uprights, and when I would get to a certain point of a sales call approaching the close, I would stand behind my desk doing kicking motions. Sometimes people in the office could see me, but it didn't matter. I just imagined the ball going through the uprights continuously. After I did that multiple times, I could achieve a state of flow. That was my personal process, but there are many different ways of getting to a state of flow.

CHAPTER 11
Process Tools

A ny state-of-the-art pitch process promoting an excellent product optimally positioned to successfully execute sales will have a strategy. When this process can be applied by strong salespeople, with positive mental attitudes, to decision-makers targeted from high probability leads, this is an even more powerful formula for driving revenues well beyond what would be possible without this combination of factors.

Creating a successful strategy will also involve the use of specific process tools. To complement all the other factors described in previous chapters, this chapter is about the process tools that make up a strong pitch process.

The security company ADP appreciates this principle and has put a lot of emphasis on training their sales team on effective sales methodologies, such as consultative selling techniques, objection handling, relationship building, and other essential sales skills.

Pitch Structure

This starts with a strong and effective sales pitch that needs to be constructed according to the following steps:

1. Understand your audience.
2. Define your unique selling proposition.
3. Craft a strong, calculated introduction or impact statement.
4. Use storytelling.
5. Address objections.
6. Create a sense of urgency.

7. Provide social proof.
8. Keep it concise and clear.
9. Practice and refine techniques and apply best practices.

Those are the building blocks of a pitch. The key to customizing this for any particular product is being able to understand, paragraph by paragraph, what to do at any given time.

If I am structuring a pitch I usually start with an introduction/impact statement, followed by some type of point of urgency, followed by qualifying to make sure that the prospect is highly likely to buy. I would follow that with features, advantages, and benefits to build value.

At a certain point, you need to introduce a price and then have a back-ended conversation after. Effective use of a variety of process tools can create fertile conditions for closing the sale. We'll get into some of the back-end process tools throughout this chapter.

Building the pitch is a very important part of the sales process. It is something that, once tested and refined, can be the driving force of any conversation. One variable is whether the pitch is by phone or face-to-face.

In a phone pitch, you are losing all your nonverbal communication cues and relying strictly on speech. Very specific tools must be in place to optimize pitching by phone. *Tone, pace,* and *pausing* are crucial, and I'll discuss those in detail in a bit.

Additionally, *active listening* is absolutely essential to make someone aware that you're paying attention even though they can't see your face. Whether that takes the form of a pause, a word of acknowledgment, or a paraphrase, these are all strong, emotive ways of being able to show active listening, as well as agreement or disagreement with certain things that are being said.

Mirroring and matching are also important. When you can't see a person's body, you can still mirror their tone or pace of speaking. You can also lead the pace by speeding it up or slowing it down so they follow you. You can create an implicit control that people don't quite understand, but which is happening and establishing who is the alpha on the call.

Use descriptive language. Paint a vivid picture with words to compensate for a lack of visual cues. Creating a way for prospects to visualize what you're describing can go a long way to making the pitch memorable and effective.

Also, do your best to exude *energy and enthusiasm*. This can be conveyed by your voice and being generally excited about a product or service, but definitely not giddy.

When you are selling face-to-face, you have several additional tools at your disposal:

- ❖ **Body language**. Maintain good posture and use power poses to appear approachable and receptive.
- ❖ **Facial expressions**. Use the face to express emotions consistent with what is being discussed at any given time.
- ❖ **Voice modulation**. Realize that verbal communication, instead of representing the full extent of your communication on a phone call, probably represents 30 or 40 percent maximum when you're face-to-face.
- ❖ **Gestures**. Use purposeful and appropriate gestures to enhance your message.
- ❖ **Eye contact**. Maintain appropriate eye contact that demonstrates sincerity, confidence, and active engagement, while being mindful of cultural differences and adapting eye contact accordingly.
- ❖ **Proximity and positioning**. Are you standing or sitting closer to convey interest and create a sense of connection? At the same time, you should respect people's personal space.

❖ **Active listening cues**. Show you are listening by nodding your head when appropriate. Also, lean forward slightly to show interest.
❖ **Dress and appearance**. Match what is expected in the industry.
❖ **Energy or enthusiasm**. Express this via body language, including facial expressions. It's important to be enthusiastic without being salesy.

There are different process tools available to salespeople to complement their pitch, depending upon whether or not they are face-to-face.

In addition to a *sales pitch*, another tool is *presentation software*. Usually, a pitch needs to hold its own, but often it can be valuable to screen-share, whether to show proprietary information or give someone a look behind the curtain.

That allows you to share *sales collateral*. This might take the form of a list of deliverables, or proprietary information. It could be a list of clients or a list of testimonials. A lot of sales collateral can be considered a process tool for sales. *Visual aids* are another tool that can be used to help a pitch. If you get into competitive analysis, they can be used to highlight what your product does compared to a competitor. Proposal templates showing where we're going to go from here can be an important tool to have on a sales pitch, if needed.

Delivery (Tone, Pace, Pausing)

Tone of voice plays a crucial role in projecting confidence, enthusiasm, and sincerity. This is how people interpret who the salesperson is. Are they of equal caliber? Are they someone who they should trust and respect? If you take away someone's eyes by pitching by phone, that is all they have to focus on. They're listening to these things to decide whether they should continue or not.

Optimizing *pace* in the sales pitch is crucial to engage the prospect and keep them from losing interest. Pace is about establishing a level of interest and knowing when to speed up to create energy and excitement and when to slow down to create anticipation, as well to emphasize a particular point. It's also about maintaining the prospect's interest level by employing contrast in the pace to improve the absorbability of the story. That's what keeps people listening and prevents their minds from drifting off.

Pauses are the third tool. This is especially important when pitching by phone with strictly verbal cues. Being comfortable with the silence that prevails during a pause establishes leadership and promotes trust and respect of the salesperson by the prospect.

Digging deeper into pitch delivery, it's important to use a positive and energetic tone, but not a needy tone. A rapport-seeking tone is looking for approval, and it's going to seem submissive. This will put you at a different level than the prospect. You don't want to be rapport-seeking with your tone. Rapport neutral would be expressing things in a normal tone and not being too abrasive or too cooperative. Choose at least a rapport-neutral tone, while showing lots of conviction, and definitely not a rapport-seeking tone.

Then there's the rapport-breaking tone, which is when you don't give up too much but really hold everything back to establish a certain power dynamic. If necessary to establish yourself as the alpha on the call, briefly shifting from a rapport-neutral tone to a tone that is more assertive or rapport-breaking can be used to regain control of the conversation. Typically, this would precede shifting back to a neutral tone where an environment of mutual respect with the prospect is best maintained.

Some people go in and out of rapport-breaking and rapport-neutral, depending on what's needed on the call. But a rapport-seeking tone tends to be used inadvertently by many salespeople, and I generally don't recommend that.

I would also recommend being confident but not pushy. It really is a balance between confidence and assertiveness. As soon as people feel that they are being pushed, they throw up strong defenses. The emotion of wanting to do something should come from within, from their own desire, as opposed to feeling like they are being forced to do something because of outside factors, or someone else's preferences.

Another tip is to speak the language of your audience. Adapting the tone to match the communication side of the audience and using language and terminology that they identify with can go a long way to being conversational and empathetic. It projects professionalism and allows you to adapt to the situation by actively listening.

These are all driving forces in choosing the right tone in the right situation to ensure that information is being delivered correctly. Tone is also what drives people's emotions, and people often buy for emotional reasons. The words can all be there, but if it just doesn't feel right, it's harder for someone to buy.

Pauses and Silences

Pausing allows you to emphasize important points. It enables you, just before a crucial statement, to present a compelling statistic. It creates anticipation and allows information to sink in, but also signals to the audience that what you're about to say is significant. These are not visual pauses. These are well-timed beats, such as pausing in an obscure place or in the middle of a sentence—almost making it seem like the salesperson lost their way before continuing. That's how one can access a deeper mindset. Just pausing in obscure places and then continuing can cause different emotional reactions by creating anticipation and desire for what comes next.

Pauses and silences can be used to highlight benefits and value. Using these techniques can (a) allow time for questions and objections, (b) break up information, (c) create suspense, (d) allow for audience reactions, (e) contribute to transitions between sections, and (f) help you practice timing and rhythm.

A good pitch with a good pace flows. It makes people feel good.

Pausing and silences can also be used to establish timing. You can pause for a long time on a cold call, for example, and not say anything for three or four seconds, and you aren't interrupted because nobody wants to be jumping in when someone is about to talk. Giving yourself enough room to think, not be rushed, or to pace yourself is a trait of good salespeople. They establish room effectively on a pitch and don't feel rushed because of the silence, which also exudes confidence.

Supplemental Questions

I would add *supplemental questions* as a way of ensuring that if we're asking questions and we don't get the right answer, we can say, "Okay, I understand." But asking the question differently is often the key to breaking through in sales.

So I would say, "And how often do you do this?" And you might say, "I do it quite often," and I would say "I see, but how many times a week, exactly?"

Asking the supplemental question to get the information you need is usually the right choice when it comes to sales. Sometimes this needs to be done to get the information required to best position the rest of the pitch and close.

At other times, it needs to be done to get the prospect to reveal something that the salesperson can use as further justification in challenging the prospect. If a nugget of information makes the prospect confident in their own mind that saying yes to the sale is the right decision, being thorough in extracting the right information is justifiable.

Some salespeople will just let something go and miss a crucial piece of information. They're not using supplemental questions as a process driver to get the information they need to create the conditions for closing the sale.

Emotionally Intelligent Pitching Decisions and Takeaways

When pitching, different factors are involved if you are doing a cold call as compared to a scheduled call.

A cold call, or an interrupting type of call, is where you get someone on the phone without them expecting your call. This kind of call has to immediately get their attention by creating value by establishing common ground, such as a client in common or awareness of a recent new product launch. This could also be established by a brief statement letting them know you have an acute awareness of a macro trend affecting their business or a potential solution to their biggest challenges. In a cold call initiated without any particular prior interaction, the prospect will be caught off guard, leading to a higher chance of resistance—i.e., skepticism. So, because there may be some upfront adversity, the call requires a higher level of resiliency, focus, and execution. You need to quickly provide the relevant details through the conversation and tailor the pitch appropriately.

Usually, this is where you need a very strong impact statement that provides the potential for the cold call to all of a sudden become a warm call—or at least one that feels solicited—because it causes the prospect to say that they really want to know more or they want to continue. If you can create that phenomenon from a cold call through a strong impact statement, the gap in efficiency of a cold call versus a scheduled call can be mostly eliminated.

But, just to compare, devoting as much time to this on a scheduled call is less necessary and may be counterproductive. Both parties have agreed on the specific time for the sales call, which allows the prospect to be mentally prepared and more receptive to the call, so, as long as the call is valuable, they're not going to cut it short. Information delivered right up front in an impact statement may be better served sprinkled later throughout the pitch as needed.

In addition to an impact statement, a cold call requires more rapport-building at first to create the right level of familiarity in a few seconds. However, communicating some points of common ground to not only generate respect but also show the prospect that this call is targeted, and not one of a hundred dials today, is a better way of generating rapport than random questions about the weather.

I will talk about false objections and how to deal with those as another process tool a few pages from now. But it's important to have a plan to get through those bumps on the road, notwithstanding a strong impact statement. Until the prospect really sees the value that you are building through the call, the call remains vulnerable.

A question that often arises is "How do you strike the right balance between persistence and respecting the other person?"

I think the answer is emotional intelligence. Too many salespeople are seen as pushy or needy because they are always closing, and they're not listening to the prospects and what they need to make an informed decision. Making sure at any given point in the sales process that the salesperson is willing to walk away adds a lot of credibility.

If someone says, "Look, I'm a little uncomfortable, I'm not sure how this could fit into our strategy," the emotionally intelligent response to that is, "Okay. Got it. This is not a problem. If it doesn't work, that's okay too. But what would you need to further understand to know whether it could be a fit?"

Always being willing to walk away and solve the problem with credibility is a world of difference from saying, "But, but, but, this will work, this is good for you" and always pushing. Setting clear expectations from the beginning that this is a two-way street—as in you have to be satisfied that it's right for you and I have to be satisfied that it's right for us—creates a foundation for mutually respectful interactions.

Then it's really about listening and observing—paying attention to cues and the signals from the prospect. If they express disinterest and ask for more time or less frequent communication, take that into account, and be willing to walk away. But it helps the process if you can find out what it is they would need to have clarity to know that this would make sense. Or even focusing on pain points and asking them how much it's going to cost them by not looking for a solution that could bring short-term ROI. There are different ways of restimulating their interest in a non-persuasive, non-pushy way.

Using a respectful tone is huge. I was talking to a friend not too long ago who was trying to do a real estate deal to get some office space, and when he said, "No"—it was almost a deal, but he didn't have the parking that he wanted in the building, and that was a deal breaker—the real estate agent said, "Okay, fine," and hung up the phone really fast. When the real estate agent eventually came back with the solution, my friend at first really didn't want to re-engage with that deal because he thought that the agent had behaved in a disrespectful, almost snippy, or flippant way.

Provide value with needed interaction. Don't waste anyone's time. There has to be a reason for every interaction or something fresh or a new angle, or something that's going to bring value. That's key to someone respecting every point of communication.

Also, offer the opportunity to opt out or not be subscribed. One of the most powerful things that you can say to someone is, "No problem. We'll take you off the list. We don't want to waste your time or ours in the future." Just offering the opportunity to opt out will often make someone say, "No, no, no, I don't want to rule this out forever. It's just not right now..."

So having the courage to be able to do these things creates a lot of credibility.

There are times to respect response times and prospect availability and times to challenge them. If someone says, "Look, I'm off the grid for the rest of the week," a salesperson has to make a decision to say, "Well, look, this is going to be gone by the time you're back," or "Look, I'll reach out to you when you're back to update you on what's happened," perhaps adding, "but I doubt it might still be available," particularly if there is a need to condition the prospect to feel some regret for not buying now.

Also, when conditioning prospects to buy on your terms in the future, you can either ask for further contacts or strategically offer to take them off the list and not contact them again. Planning ways to go back to the prospect with a fresh opportunity is important, whether transparently suggested or strategically hidden from the prospect. Building trust is important, but the element of surprise can be another way of creating future sales with someone who failed to buy previously. Be transparent, reliable, and consistent, but it's always possible to come up with a good reason to reapproach a prospect under slightly adjusted circumstances to create a future sale, whether they are expecting it or not. Doing what you say you're going to do to create a culture of trust is important.

On the other hand, if there is a time limit on a prospect's decision, credibility will be lost if the salesperson promises, at the request of the prospect, to reach back out with the same deal in the future. As such, it is okay to agree to reach back out in an upcoming quarter, but conditioning the prospect to know that the same deal is off the table and that the purpose of the future contact is more about something else, like "seeing what is possible or not" with future product offerings.

Objection Handling (True and False)

False objections will typically come up early on a cold or interrupting call. False objections are things that people are going to say until they're convinced they should have the conversation. Sometimes people will say, "I'm busy" or "I'm in a meeting." Sometimes they will tell you to speak to someone else. Sometimes, they'll say, "Send me some information" or "What's the price?"

I call these false objections because, depending on what your product is, they usually don't even know what you're calling about yet, and they can't assess the value. So, in theory, these objections don't really matter if you pitch the way I've described. If you are building value with every sentence, what will usually happen, once the right amount of value is created, is that the false objection will be forgotten and prospects will then start listening rather than objecting to get you off the phone.

There are different ways of managing those false objections. You can address them, but because you have a limited amount of time, there are diminishing returns to doing that.

Your pitch is like the home-field advantage in sports—you want to be on your home field where possible. If you allow the prospect to say, "Well, wait a second, is this one of those products that do x and y?" it can allow them to redefine the call. Then they take over the home field and make you stop or go off your pitch. That's giving them the home-field advantage, and we don't want to do that.

Usually, I would recommend acknowledging the false objection early in the pitch, then getting right back into your prepared pitch. It's similar to, in football, faking right and going left when you're trying to shake off the defender. It's almost like the prospect thinks that you're answering their question, and by the time they realize that you haven't, they've forgotten about it, or you have built enough value to accommodate it.

If it comes up again, you might hear, "That's very interesting, but I want you to talk to somebody else." Saying, "Not a problem," or "Absolutely" but continuing with the pitch will probably remedy that situation a lot of the time once you have enough value built into the pitch.

If it comes up a third time, you probably have to address it, and you probably have to do a little bit of a power play. "Look, I appreciate you want me to talk to someone else, but I'm not inviting them. I'm speaking to you, and I don't even know yet if you qualify," or something similar. There's a way of being able to handle it like you're riding a bucking bronco or a bull that's trying to throw you off its back.

There are ways of managing those situations until you can stabilize by communicating value through the pitch. Arguably, depending upon what you're pitching, that may be a better strategy than being submissive or just giving up all power and dealing with the agenda of the other person— because all false objections really do is stop us from getting to the critical place where we're creating value and can actually have a business conversation.

If you are playing the numbers game, the more someone can get to the point of value where they can have a business conversation following their pitch, the more opportunities are created—and a greater percentage of those pitch opportunities will close. But you cannot do that in an emotionally unintelligent way. You need to be clever, and you need to be able to manage and appease the emotions of the person on the other end of the phone to do that effectively.

It's all about frame control and on-platform pitching.

Pitch Anything by Oren Klaff talks an awful lot about frame control and how there can only be one frame and one winner of the frame. In many ways, what I'm recommending in terms of dealing with false objections corresponds with that approach. Once you get into a critical part of the pitch— maybe that's after price, maybe that's once you are established through some trial closing questions—you reach a point where you want to deal with objections, because true objections are good. Any seasoned salesperson is probably going to tell you that they never closed anyone who didn't have any objections.

When you are dealing with true objections, there are several ways to manage them. One way would be by using *accusation audits*, a phrase coined by Chris Voss in *Never Split the Difference*. According to Voss, an accusation audit is a form of emotional labeling that involves calling out your counterpart's negative emotions potentially about *you* specifically. An accusation audit aims to trigger empathy in your opponent and diffuse tension by putting it all out there in the open. One could say in response to an objection "It seems like I'm frustrating you" and call out the elephants in the room. Without even addressing the objections, this approach can force them to the surface to get them to go away. That's one style of objection handling.

The true objection-handling process that I have used the most is also one I learned when I was a professional mediator early in my career. It corresponds to best practices in applied mediation where you would always begin, when facing a real objection, by empathizing with the objection as a starting point. This shows the prospect that you can see it their way and walk a few steps in their shoes. In addition to creating trust and mutual respect, it establishes a collaborative approach to potentially resolving any objections.

The next step in the process would be to *isolate the objections* to find other objections. This is because objections are not mutually exclusive. Often, we can solve multiple objections with one attempt rather than trying to overcome them right away or one by one: "Okay, I appreciate your knowing that there is the right amount of value to justify this is important to you. Apart from price, are there any other reasons you wouldn't want to do this?" Hopefully this will lead to the prospect disclosing other objections.

If you can go from one objection to three, four, or five objections to get everything on the table, there's now the possibility of resolving the obstacles collectively, as opposed to individually. There's a lot of power in that. It's similar to bowling when you roll one ball and you knock down ten pins. That would be optimized objection handling, so best not to bowl the ball until multiple pins are exposed and lined up—until, that is, you are ready to overcome all the objections, which is the fifth and final step in the process, and premature at this point.

Number 3 in the process once you get all those objections on the table, you will want to *clarify the objections*. Break them down into smaller and smaller pieces. I call it chewing your food. An objection is like eating a piece of cake. You're not going to just swallow the piece of cake whole. You need to break it down.

To clarify a price objection, for example, you could say as a starting point, "Look, I can appreciate that it's not inexpensive, but is it that you don't see the value, or is it that you don't have the budget?" Different solutions would apply depending on the prospect's answer. "What else would you need to understand to justify the expense?"

The next clarifying part of the pitch is where we do smart questioning, which we'll get into in a bit. You can ask ROI questions or about growth and pro-growth strategies, and about comparing to other alternatives.

After you have clarified and broken down the objections into smaller pieces, where they're not mutually exclusive, there's an opportunity in the fourth step of objection handling to *ask a conditional close question*. Often, that requires being indifferent and saying, "Okay, look, maybe we'll solve this. Maybe we won't. But if we could figure out A, B and C [objections], would it be perfectly obvious you'd want to do this?" If you get a yes to that, then you've contained all the objections. If you get a no to that, then maybe there's a hidden objection under the skin—a splinter or something that got buried. So you need to say, "Okay, well, look, maybe we won't get this done. But why not?" Then you ask again, and you go through the process again to get all the objections out.

Doing that almost creates a warp speed of problem-solving like in *Star Wars or Star Trek, when they press the hyperspace or warp-speed button.* When we use this type of methodology, in sales we have an opportunity to solve all existing problems in an accelerated, systematic way, and close conditionally.

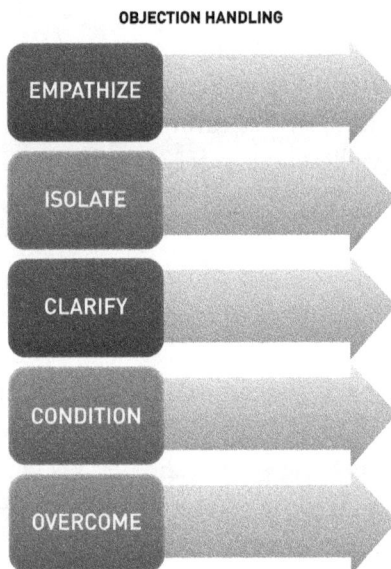

OBJECTION HANDLING

EMPATHIZE

ISOLATE

CLARIFY

CONDITION

OVERCOME

Step 5 of the process would be to *overcome*. But I often say that unless it's a one-call close, that's the least important thing, especially following an initial pitch on a two, three, or more call-closing strategy. If someone can get to that step of the process, then I can involve someone with a bit more experience to close. Then maybe we set up this next call and make solving the objections with transparency and evidence the purpose of the call. Setting it up so that prospects attend the next call to have their objections resolved rather than having looming objections stop people from joining the next call is key to this process.

As discussed previously, understanding the prospect's decision-making process is also important in setting up the next call. You could ask: "What's your decision-making process? Who needs to be involved? If others need to be involved, it will be important for everyone to attend the next call to see if we can reconcile this." Involving others with a say in the decision in future calls is important in creating fertile conditions for generating a yes.

Salespeople must optimize that particular process to get through the turbulence of false objections, get into the back end, frame the conditions under which something could close, and do that with multiple opportunities. If they can do all that, sales would be predictable. Then, after applying state-of-the-art processes consistently, generating predictable sales becomes mostly a numbers game. Making optimized choices in handling objections is a key part of the process to expeditiously generate sales.

Smart Questioning

Smart questioning is the engine of transformation in sales and can be applied at multiple points in the sales process. I've frequently done smart-questioning training for people. As I mentioned in the introduction, I was visited at one point in London by Alan Shepard, the former president of Concordia University. That's when we had the conversation that led me to realize why business schools don't cater to sales and why there's no fifth discipline in it. After that, I was invited back to Concordia University to give a seminar on smart questioning to internal salespeople responsible, amongst other things, for fundraising, and some MBA professors. At the time I attributed the interest by a diverse audience to the fact that there's not a lot of material written about the subject.

This could easily be a topic for another book, so I won't get into everything. But often I will ask people how many different types of questions there are, and they will usually start with two. They'll say there are open-ended and closed-ended questions. Then I say, "Okay, that's true. What if I told you that most open-ended questions and most closed-ended questions could be asked in a positive or negative way?"

An example of a positive closed-ended question might be "Is this something you would want to do?" Whereas negative versions might be, "Is there a reason you wouldn't want to do this?" or "Isn't this something you would want to avoid?"

We can also make open-ended questions positive or negative. "Could you please share insights into the challenges you've faced in meeting deadlines consistently on your projects?" Or "Can you explain why you consistently fail to meet deadlines on your projects?"

Negative questions often lead to positive responses, and positive questions the opposite. "Sounds like everything is perfect in your business" may elicit a reply "Well, I wouldn't say everything is perfect." Positive questions are often likely to elicit negative responses. For example, without enough built trust, a question such as "What are some of the problems in your business?" might shut down a prospect and yield a response (depending on the level of trust established by the salesperson) such as "No, we don't have a lot of problems in our business."

There are other types of questions. There are *fact*-based questions that allow you to establish the fundamentals. "How many offices do you have?" "How many employees do you have?" That can also be used to create a level of truthful dialogue with prospects. After all, such questions do not allow for much interpretation since they are either true or not and can often be easily verified.

There are *pain*-point questions that involve understanding people's frustration. "How frustrating is it to know that there are customers for you everywhere that you can't even get in front of?"

Then you can ask an *implication* question, which would be, "If there were a way to get you in front of more customers, what impact would that have on your business?"

Then a solution/*need* question would let you explain how those requirements relate to your product: "If we could create a system for getting you in front of more qualified customers, would it be perfectly obvious you would want us to work together?"

Those four types of questions—fact (situation), pain, implication, solution (need)—combined in that order are sometimes referred to as "spin selling." This is the title of a book by Neil Rapin, which is about how to use different styles and combinations of questions to create a transformative experience in the mind of a prospect.

There are many other types of questions. There are reverse-sell questions to get a prospect telling you why they're good. There are compare-and-contrast questions to help distinguish other ways the prospect could go about solving things on their own from solutions that your product offers. There are trial close questions. (We'll get into closing in the next chapter.) Closing questions can be assumptive, direct, conditional, and so on. Through practice, the best salespeople have learned these styles of questions and a variety of unique combinations and know when to use them strategically to bridge the gap between where someone is and where they need to be to close the sale.

I tell ambitious salespeople, who want to become as good as they possibly can, that they're going to need to learn smart questioning at the same level that they learned the alphabet or their times tables. A lot of practice has to go into recognizing the best question to ask at any given time. The salesperson who asks the best questions tends to be the one who's going to close the most deals and make the most money. It's kind of like a rowing team, eight rowers pushing forward and covering massive amounts of ground with each stroke. That's the propulsion that smart questioning should create. Whereas dud questions that go nowhere will cause stagnation that slows progress toward the sale.

When someone can ask three or four questions in a way that is almost like a one-two-three punch in boxing, it is far more powerful than just throwing up random questions that don't really accomplish anything, Such a combination of purposeful questions builds a bridge to where you need to get in pursuit of the sale. The very best salespeople can make forecasts about getting the sale past the finish line: "I can close this deal in three or four questions" or "These are building blocks for conclusions that the prospect needs to consider." in order to close.

Urgency

Urgency in sales refers to time sensitivity in the sales opportunity, and its importance in sales has been mentioned throughout this book. It is designed to convey to the prospect the need for prompt action, allowing the salesperson to use timing leverage during the sales process. It's the ability to convey to the potential customer that there is a pressing reason to decide sooner rather than later. This is often driven by consequences; sometimes, it can be sweetened with incentives.

A sense of urgency can be an effective sales technique to motivate customers to take action and is a fundamental element of everything that is sold. As explained in an earlier chapter, if you go to a retail store with products on sale, the incentive for someone to buy now may be savings of 50 percent, but the consequence is that the sale expires tomorrow. So there's an incentive and a consequence when it comes to applied urgency.

All products associated with sales need some form of urgency to add value because sales can only add value if it speeds up the time frame in which people buy. Strategies to create urgency include limited-time offers, a set deadline, or a promotion emphasizing limited availability or limited stock, all of which highlight the consequences of inaction and demonstrate value when customers can receive immediate benefits from a product.

I have friends who have sold complicated supply chain systems to hospitals, and their strategic use of urgency was often limited to "If you start today, you're going to start benefiting from the ROI, savings, and convenience of our products sooner." This can be seen as a milder form of urgency compared to "If you don't buy now, we will allocate the product to another customer and you will need to wait it out until we finally get caught up with our production."

Mild versus extreme points of urgency are not always going to apply to every product since many points of urgency will likely fall somewhere in between. Having a strategy around urgency and being able to build that strategy into the sales pitch and make it perfectly believable is essential. You don't want to create urgency for nothing and not have it shorten your sales cycle, or be exaggerated or inconsistent, and be seen as dishonest.

As I have said several times in this book, people want things that they can't have, and people value things that are scarce. This is something that needs to be built in correctly for every product to make sales most effective in reducing the time that prospects take to buy.

If, when you're making a pitch, someone says, "Look, I don't really think I can make a commitment to your product right now," you need to respond in an emotionally intelligent way and say, "Okay, maybe this isn't going to work now, but notwithstanding the timeframe, what would you need further from me to have the clarity to decide whether this is something you would want to do?" as opposed to "You need this product so you will still need to decide now."

The latter response is more of an ultimatum and can work at times, potentially to call a bluff, but more frequently would likely get a firm no, whereas the former response breaks down the timing objection in a way that could reveal solutions without your losing credibility.

Urgency is not pressure and, if used correctly, will create desire from within, as opposed to external pressure. It's not "Buy this car or else..." Putting pressure on someone may work on occasion, but it's unsustainable.

Credibility is an important part of understanding what is needed to motivate someone, in an emotionally intelligent way, to see things differently or do things differently.

Indifference is a part of it, too. Much like the example I used earlier in the book, I can say, "If we're going to do this, we need to do this today." That could feel like pressure until I add, "but if not, that's okay too." Indifference relieves the pressure of the urgency situation like letting air out of an overly inflated tire.

CHAPTER 12

Closing

Preparing for the Close

The process of closing sales is the final stage, where the salesperson seeks to secure a commitment from the prospect to make a purchase. It involves guiding the prospect toward a buying decision and overcoming any final objections or hesitation. This chapter will cover closing from the perspective of a salesperson mindset and process, as well as providing a list of commonly used closing questions.

This section features a summary of the steps typically involved in closing a sale, which include:

1. **Recognizing buying signals**. The salesperson should be attentive to signs that indicate the prospect's readiness to buy, such as questions about pricing, delivery, or product specifications, as well as positive body language or verbal cues.

2. **Addressing objections**. As described previously, it is critical to address any objections or concerns through actively listening, empathizing, and providing relevant information or solutions to alleviate any doubts.

3. **Presenting options**. This is a bit controversial because some sales processes require only one option to avoid confusion If required by the approach taken in pursuing the sale, providing options, such as hypotheticals (described later in this chapter), can help prospects feel empowered in their decision, increasing the chances of closing the sale.

4. **Asking for the sale**. Once objections are addressed and suitable options are presented, the salesperson should ask for the prospect's commitment to make a purchase using an appropriate closing question.

5. **Overcoming hesitation**. The salesperson should listen attentively and provide information or reassurance to address these concerns while closing and re-closing.

6. **Confirming the sale**. The salesperson should guide the close once the prospect has agreed to discuss the details of the sale by recording key facts and solidifying the closing moments by gathering the right information and making sure that commitment is secured.

Closing Questions

It's hard to know exactly how many types of closing questions there are. Below, I've listed eighteen types that can be applied to different situations. We'll focus on some of the most important ones from the list later in the chapter.

List of Closing Questions

❖ **Direct close**. For example, "Is this something you want to do?"

❖ **Alternative close**. "Would you prefer the basic package or a premium package?" This type of close is also assumptive.

❖ **Trial close**. We'll go into this in a bit more detail shortly. For example, "How do you feel about this product or service so far?" There are ways of trial closing throughout the whole process in order to assess where the prospect is. It's about getting feedback as opposed to forcing the prospect to make the decision prematurely.

❖ **Summary close**. This is something that would come into play after going through a lot of information. "Is what we have discussed as a solution aligning with your needs?"

❖ **Objection close**. "Now that I've explained our return policy, does that alleviate your concerns about the product quality?"

❖ **Urgency close**. "This special promotion ends tomorrow, so is it something you would like to do?" This close is also direct.

❖ **Cost comparison close**. "When you consider the long-term benefit, would you agree that our product or services are actually more cost effective?" This question is also leading.

❖ **FOMO close**. For example, "Many customers have already taken advantage of this opportunity. Would this be something you would want to join them in doing?"

❖ **I need satisfaction close**. "Does the solution meet all your requirements and address your problems?"

❖ **Agreement close**. "Can we both agree that our product or services would be a valuable addition to your business?"

❖ **Final thought close**. "Is there anything else you need to know before making a decision?"

❖ **Future-oriented close**. "If you were to implement the solution, how do you envision it benefiting your business in the long run?"

❖ **ROI close**. "Based on the potential return on investment, would it make sense to proceed with this purchase?"

❖ **Referral close**. "Do you know anyone else who might benefit from this product or service?"

- ❖ **Collaboration close**. "How can we work together to ensure seamless implementation of the solution?"
- ❖ **Follow up close**. "When should I reach out to you again to discuss the next step?"
- ❖ **Social proof close**. "You have seen a lot of customers sharing positive feedback about the product/service. Are you ready to join them?"
- ❖ **Value proposition close**. "Considering the unique features and benefits, would you agree that our product or service offers exceptional value?" This is another leading question.

These are just examples of closing questions. Which of them you use depends on the context of the customer relationship and individual experience. So it's important to adapt.

It also depends on style because often, if we are doing a resistance sale, being too leading or assumptive can break the frame of *who is the prize*. We really need to be consistent with that style. If someone is taking more of a friendly, cooperative approach, they could be saying things like "Wouldn't you agree?" but that's definitely quite leading.

If the frame is more resistant, you might want to be more neutral to avoid driving the objections underground and say, "Would it make sense for you to do this or not?" Give them the option to opt in or opt out and not hide their objections by forcing them to say yes when there might be a lingering objection in their mind.

You really want to be conscious of what styles are used as closing questions are asked.

Always Be Closing

In the first part of the chapter, we talked a little bit about when closing happens, but arguably, closing is always happening. I take a bit here from the movie *Glengarry Glen Ross,* which I referenced earlier in the book. There's an adage called "always be closing" (ABC), which is commonly used in sales and was popularized by the 1992 film.

It emphasizes the importance of continually pursuing the goal of furthering, upholding, and closing the sale throughout the entire sales process. The phrase is sometimes misunderstood because good closing requires a buildup of momentum and a regrouping strategy with every closing attempt, making the next attempt more promising.

The phrase suggests that a salesperson should have a constant mindset focused on seeking opportunities to move the customer closer to making a purchasing decision. Rather than viewing the sales process as a series of separate steps or interactions, the ABC approach encourages salespeople to continually work toward closing the deal.

This embodies several key principles:

- ❖ Utilize active engagement.
- ❖ Build rapport.
- ❖ Identify opportunities.
- ❖ Prepare to overcome objections.
- ❖ Ask for the sale.

This whole approach encourages persistence, but it is crucial to balance persistence with being customer-centric and aware of what is occurring in the mind of the prospect. Professional salespeople should focus on providing value, understanding customer needs, and ensuring a positive buying experience. Pushing too aggressively or using manipulative tactics can be counterproductive and damage the chances of closing the sale. The concept of ABC needs to be an undercurrent in the mind of the salesperson rather than an in-your-face approach. This is enabled by salespeople focusing throughout the sale on what I call a trial close.

Trial closes are indirect ways of getting perspective and feedback from the customer as to where they are at any given time. Their use helps salespeople avoid seeming pushy by trying to close a sale too soon.

Becoming a Closer

I'm often asked if a salesperson should strive to do it all—from prospecting to closing or if there is a particular role in sales for an independent closer.

Becoming a closer is not just about developing into a better salesperson. They're two very different roles. It's a bit like someone learning to be a great pitcher and a great hitter in baseball. In some ways, they're interrelated, but ultimately, they're very different skill sets.

What I have found when developing salespeople is that, as a logical sequence to laying the groundwork for becoming a closer, I need to get them focused on the fundamentals of prospecting, pitching, and creating opportunities. In my experience, I may not have had people closing for one, two, or three years sometimes and having other people supplementing their sales to help them close. Then a certain percentage of people will develop into closers and can help other people close sales and become closers themselves. When someone becomes a closer, they typically focus on the final stages of the sales process and use specific techniques and skills to close sales. Closers tend to have advanced negotiation skills and product knowledge and rely on specific processes such as the use of closing questions and urgency to structure their approach.

Some people are happy being very good salespeople and just prospecting. They focus on creating the conditions for other people to help them close. It really depends on the strategy. If it's a less sophisticated sale or value proposition, it might be easier to combine the two roles.

However, in more complex sales, there's significant value in bringing in a second voice, someone who's going to say the same type of thing but from a different perspective and with the purpose of closing. Distinguishing and keeping these roles separate is quite important because as people become better and better at pitching and they hear closers saying brilliant things to close their deals, some of these things tend to leak into their conversations. When this happens, they're stealing the thunder of the closer or creating conditions where they're answering too many questions before the closer gets involved, resulting in the prospect often making the decision in between meetings or in between calls. If the prospect calls off the final meeting, then the closer doesn't get the opportunity to play their role and add value by closing the sale.

What I tell salespeople in such cases is that you're either playing the role of the dental hygienist—i.e., sales prospecting—or the dentist—i.e., sales closing. You're not both. What you need to do is create a pitch opportunity and set up a second call for the closer to get involved. You may be good enough to spot the cavities, but that's not your job when you are the dental hygienist or salesperson in prospecting mode. Your job is to clean the teeth, prepare the teeth, get everything ready so the dentist can come in and do their part. You really have to be disciplined enough to resist the temptation of doing what the dentist does. Many salespeople become very good at being able to close their own sales over time as well. But closing is a much more challenging art than pitching, and it tends to take people longer to learn that skill set.

Primary Closing Questions: Trial, Conditional, Direct, Assumptive

Trial close questions are typically seeded throughout the pitch to get real-time feedback on what's being presented without necessarily asking for the business directly. You want to use trial close questions before the prospect is ready to buy because prematurely asking questions more specific to closing can be counterproductive. Doing so is kind of like trying to open a green banana. It doesn't open very easily, so it does not make sense to force it open. It has to ripen and develop before you ask that type of question, because it might not be appropriate at that moment.

Forcing the prospect to focus on the wrong conclusion before completing the groundwork could be counterproductive to closing the sale. An incorrectly placed direct closing question might stand out as being asked at an inappropriate time, forcing a no, and could hurt the credibility of the salesperson, as well as any trust and respect that has been established.

Following are some examples of trial close questions. I'll contrast this with other more developed closing questions from the list such as direct closes and conditional closes. Here are some trial close examples:

- ❖ "Could you see the supplying of our product working to your advantage?"
- ❖ "Would you gain perspective on how our involvement would benefit your business if I could arrange a live demonstration?"
- ❖ "Do you think our product or service would be a good fit for your need or not really?"
- ❖ "Would you consider gaining the advantages created by our product a priority for your business?"
- ❖ "When you're targeting new customers, do you prospect regionally or are you looking for new clients all across the United States?"
- ❖ "How would you see this product working for you?"
- ❖ "What are the key factors you're considering when choosing a new vendor?"

- ❖ "Can you envision how our product or service would benefit your organization in terms of cost savings and efficiency gained?"
- ❖ "Do you have any specific concerns that would stop you from moving forward?"
- ❖ "What would be the timeline for implementation if you were to proceed with the product or service, based on our discussion today?"
- ❖ "What do you see as the next step in moving forward?"

These are all softer questions designed to get the prospect to give feedback that will contribute to the momentum in pursuing a path toward closing throughout the entire sales process. The purpose of trial close questions is to assess the prospect's interest and their readiness to make a decision, to gather insight and address any concerns or objections.

Probing questions also focus on timing and are typically used throughout the sales process, starting in the discovery phase and continuing until the final closing stage. It allows you to ask the following examples:

- ❖ "Does our product or service meet your requirements?"
- ❖ "What do you think about the benefits we discussed so far?"
- ❖ "If we were able to offer you some special conditions, would that make a difference in your decision?"
- ❖ "If we were able to provide you with some references or case studies with satisfied customers, would that help you in the process of making an informed decision?"
- ❖ "If we were able to fully address your concerns, would you be ready to move forward?"

These last three questions have the attributes of both trial and conditional close questions.

These types of well-tailored trial questions need to be delivered in an emotionally intelligent way at the right time to be most effective. They need to be used in the context of what's happening in the moment to come up with that perfect question. The goal is to slice open the idea in the mind of the prospect, in a neutral way that's not threatening, and encourage them to think through the idea as a byproduct of answering the question thoughtfully. That's really where these powerful questions come into play, because they are going to generate better answers. This will help propel the prospect forward in their thinking in hopes of bridging the gap between where they are and where the salesperson wants to take them to close the sale.

Although there are on occasion some common attributes, unlike the indirect approach provided by trial close questions, conditional close questions are used by salespeople to pivot from existing objections to understanding whether their resolution could help complete the sale.

When conditionally closing, salespeople have a requirement that needs to be met in order for their prospects to move forward with purchases. This condition could be related to budget or time, for instance, or other factors or sets of objections that might influence the buying decision.

Conditional closing questions take a set of circumstances and pull them together. In a resistance-type sale, it can be quite effective because, as discussed before, you may be handling objections by empathizing and isolating objections and then clarifying them. When you clarify them, you break down all the circumstances, then reassemble them in a conditional statement that could actually be used to elicit a yes. I might ask a conditional close question positively: "Maybe this will work. Maybe it won't. But if we could take care of A, B and C [i.e., identified objections], would this be something you would want to do?" Or I could ask that same conditional close question negatively: "Maybe this will work. Maybe it won't.

But if we could take care of A, B and C, would there be any other reason you wouldn't want to do this?"

Those conditional close questions can be very powerful in establishing a set of circumstances that is going to allow the prospect to catch up emotionally with the conclusions that have been reached throughout the process.

Another type of closing question is a direct close. A direct close offers a straightforward and explicit approach for the salesperson to directly ask the prospect to make a purchase. This technique cuts to the chase, leaving no room for hesitation. The salesperson may ask a question such as "Do you want to do this? or "Is this something you want to do?" It is about asking an extremely direct question. The intention is to be assertive and concise and present the value of product benefits while asking directly for the sale. This approach will be effective in situations where the prospect is already highly interested, ready to make a decision, and just needs a little nudge to get across the finish line.

These are questions that would come when you're at the eleventh hour or when you have to galvanize a bunch of ideas. This is when closing questions are most important because if not done correctly, you can discuss many issues and points that leave a lot of ideas floating around in the mind of a prospect like loose tentacles drifting in the ocean with no real purpose or conclusion.

The closing question is what galvanizes an end to the inconclusiveness of unresolved ideas and creates conclusions in the prospect's mind that are both powerful and sticky. There is an emotional experience that takes place, chemicals that fire in their brain, and the whole experience of choosing closing questions at the right point will contribute to that.

Sometimes it's important to be able to shock them with something that abrupt and that blunt. Sometimes it's very appropriate to use a direct close because that's what's necessary to galvanize those conclusions. Sometimes you just need to be a little bit more direct. If a conditional close question will help the salesperson know if all objections have been identified and a direct close question might either lead to a sale or expose other objections, an assumptive close might be a better option if it just feels right and everything's moving along swimmingly. "Would you be signing the paperwork, or would you want it to be Bill or Peter or Sally?"

The assumptive close refers to a sales technique where the salesperson assumes the prospect has already decided to purchase the product or service instead of asking the prospect if they want to buy it. The salesperson makes statements or asks questions that imply the sale is already confirmed. This approach is based on the assumption that by presenting the buying process as a natural step, the prospect will feel more inclined to agree and complete the purchase. This is a tactic used to create a sense of confidence and urgency, encouraging the prospect to move forward with the sale.

There's also an awful lot going on in people's minds when you ask a pure closing question that is not perceived as manipulative by the prospect. This is where emotions can play a huge role in determining whether someone buys or not. When you ask an original closing question, one that does not seem leading or self-serving, it may take a millisecond to blaze a new route through the circuitry of a prospect's mind. The conclusion reached evokes an emotional response, forming a habit based on chemicals firing in the prospect's mind.

If you ask the following conditional close question, "If we could take care of A, B and C, would it be perfectly obvious you would want to do this?" and the answer is "Yeah, under those conditions, I do think I would want to do this," that answer is powerful because it locks in the conclusion—for the prospect, it is the closest thing to a habit in relation to the unique set of circumstances contained in the conditional close question.

These types of conclusions are sticky and can be locked in and restimulated at different times in the sales process, which is a huge advantage for salespeople who are aware of this phenomenon.

It's a bit like rock climbing. When rock climbers scale a rock face, after a certain amount of progress, they will lock in, which means they are not going to fall any lower than where they've locked themselves in. The analogy between rock climbers locking into the rock face and salespeople making progress toward closing the sale and locking in their progress with strong closing questions describes this phenomenon well. If done well, these choices shape the way the prospect looks at the opportunity in the moment and in the future.

Hypotheticals

One question that often arises is how salespeople can use hypotheticals to test how changing variables will create a difference in the conclusion and outcomes of a prospect's buying decision. Hypothetical scenarios are a way of canvassing what would be the right combination of circumstances to create a close. These are some of the factors:

Understand the process. Analyze the current situation before introducing hypothetical scenarios. You should have a solid understanding of the process with regard to current business environment challenges and goals, which ensures that hypotheticals are relevant and tailored to their specific needs.

Identify key variables that could impact the prospect's buying decision. These variables can include market competitors, regulatory changes, technological advancements, or any other factors that are relevant to their industry. You might ask how they would respond or adapt to changes, what strategy they would implement, or what potential risks or opportunities they foresee. There's a lot to learn by shaking the tree in that way. Make sure to listen closely to their responses. Their answers can provide valuable insights into their decision-making process, their level of adaptability, and their priorities.

Tailor your pitch and solutions based on a prospect's response. Tailor the pitch and solutions in line with their specific concerns or goals, and highlight how your product or service could help to navigate and thrive in different scenarios by mitigating risk or capitalizing on opportunities or providing flexibility.

Provide evidence of data to back up claims. Support recommendations with evidence or data. Utilize case studies, industry reports, success stories, and anecdotes to demonstrate how your solution has helped other clients overcome similar challenges and adapt to changing circumstances.

Address objections or uncertainty. Address objections and uncertainties about hypothetical scenarios directly by providing additional information, clarifying any misinterpretations, and offering reassurance to build confidence in your proposed solutions.

This is a more complex close because it will be used when a one or two-dimensional proposal is just not creating the value or the conclusions that someone needs in order to make an affirmative buying decision. Introducing another variable through hypotheticals or a series of variables could create a yes from a no, just from looking at the range of possibilities in any given closing situation.

Using Objections to Create Closing Opportunities

You can leverage objections as opportunities to further engage prospects and ultimately close sales. There are several ways to achieve this:

One is *active listening.* When prospects raise objections, listen attentively to their concerns and acknowledge their viewpoint. Showing that you value their input demonstrates empathy and clarifies objections. Seek clarification by asking open-ended questions and encouraging prospects to elaborate on their objections. This helps the salesperson understand the root cause and gain deeper insights into their concerns.

Provide concise answers that address specific concerns raised and provide relevant information, data, testimonials, and support to alleviate any doubts or hesitation. This should be considered in relation to the objection-handling process I described in the previous chapter, which discourages people from overcoming objections in an adversarial manner, like it's a debate. What you don't want is for someone to have an objection that is dismissed by the salesperson, leading to a conflict and a dead-end in the sale.

In order to use objections to create closing opportunities, gather more information first, then institute a process for overcoming them at the right moment once they have stewed for a while and once you have enough information on the table. At that point, it's important to address the objections directly and see if resolving them creates a clear path to the prospect wanting to buy.

Often, objections give you a chance to provide additional value and information about how your product or service can address their concerns and overcome perceived drawbacks. Agree that the prospect's objection is valid, and provide alternative solutions and demonstrate flexibility by providing other options, adding some extra value if appropriate in the form of a conditional closing tool to meet specific needs or preferences.

Provide social proof. We've talked about this a lot. Testimonial studies are often going to make those objections evaporate like a snowball on a warm day. Show real-life examples to create that comfort level. In some types of sales, a trial or pilot program might be the appropriate way to bridge the gap between a big objection and getting someone to take a step in the right direction. If the objection is related to uncertainty or risk, a trial period or a pilot program can often alleviate that risk without a full commitment.

Close with confidence. Once you have addressed the objections, it's most likely time to ask for the sale. Explain the benefits of your products or services and ask if they're ready to move forward. As we've discussed, many different closing questions could be asked in that particular situation.

Follow up with the prospect. Address their objections and agree on a follow-up plan, schedule, call, or meeting. Provide additional information, address any remaining concerns, and offer further support in the decision-making process. Then ask for the sale again by introducing new elements and mixing it up and shaking the tree. Often a no will become a yes, just on the basis of moving through the process of considering different variables in conjunction with core issues.

To add to what I've said earlier, I remember, when I started to close, having a really interested prospect on the line. My manager, who had been doing my closing, wasn't around, so I just closed the deal myself—that's more or less how I learned to close, drawing upon what I had observed previously from my manager. Then the next time she wasn't around and someone else on the team had a need to close, they asked me to do it, and before I knew it, I was a closer. It basically happened organically and as a result of my stepping up when the opportunities presented themselves. That's how it often tends to happen.

But, realistically, what we need to do most of the time is throw closing opportunities to the A team. Sure, things can occur by accident. It's awesome when that happens, and it creates individual and organizational growth. But there are also programs to help prepare people to be in those situations. So salespeople can learn to close effectively through different strategies. Various resources that can put people on the road to closing even before they're given the responsibility include the following:

- ❖ Attending sales training programs, courses and workshops
- ❖ Seeking mentorship and guidance from experienced professionals
- ❖ Reading books, articles, blogs on sales techniques, negotiation skills, and closing strategy
- ❖ Taking advantage of online courses and webinars
- ❖ Studying successful salespeople or industry experts
- ❖ Seeking feedback from sales managers, colleagues or customers
- ❖ Participating in industry conferences and networking events

Mastering the art of closing takes time and practice. To become a successful closer, remain open to learning about techniques and to engaging with new situations that continually refine skills. With that said, there are some drawbacks to the process.

Over the years, we've tried a few times to institute programs to take our best salespeople and accelerate their journey to becoming master closers. At one point, there was a program that top salespeople took that was delivered by a group based in the mortgage industry. They were renowned for closing a lot of sales in a B2C environment. The program turned out to be a disaster. We put some of our best people in this program and sales for many kind of dried up, in part because there were some contradictory principles more in line with persuasive sales introduced during this training. We discovered there was confusion about best practices.

Sometimes that has to do with knowing what your sales approach is, and making sure that any material introduced does not contradict it. The reason is that some styles of closing are inconsistent, so when they're applied, they are incongruent with how a prospect may have been originally approached.

Most of the time, the prospect is going to see the contradiction in that, even if it's quite subtle.

I remember another time when we brought in an alleged master closer to try to teach closing in his style. It quickly became apparent that a lot of this style was innate and not teachable, and it just created too much confusion—most people could neither replicate his style nor institutionalize the decisions suggested into a series of explainable steps.

So we went back to the KISS principle—"Keep it simple, stupid." When trying to intervene in and accelerate people's journey to becoming master closers, it's often better to take the slow route and have them learn it from the ground up. In my case, as I described, I happened to be in the right place at the right time. That gave me an opportunity to close. My desire allowed me to apply a state-of-the-art methodology that was consistent with how salespeople prospecting were setting up closing opportunities. And before I knew it, I had a team of people who I was closing for, because it just happened organically. Later, it became evident that this closing methodology was transferable to other people, which led to the creation of many other closers. But there are other times when we have to teach people how to do that more gradually.

Another issue is teaching people how to close over the phone, relying only on the verbal approach that we've talked about. When we do that, it's a whole different experience than when we introduce them to closing face-to-face. As explained earlier in the book, when comparing prospecting by phone to prospecting face-to-face, many different dynamics come into play. There are pros and cons to both, and there are things that only using your words can do to help people learn to close quickly without any distractions. People can become almost anything they want to be when they have the advantage of the prospect only hearing their voice.

Face-to-face closing does allow other means of communication that enable people to absorb what someone is saying to a higher degree, because you gain the benefit of the nonverbal. But there are also traps where prospects can observe the salesperson's facial expressions, their clothes, their mannerisms, and general demeanor.

There are many more ways for a prospect to pick someone apart when they're seeing them than when they're talking over the phone. There are different dynamics when it comes to selling over the phone versus selling face-to-face.

There's another important piece to do with asking for the sale. This is just an observation that I've gleaned over the years. I could have a salesperson on the left who sounds better, who is having more comprehensive conversations than the salesperson on the right. Everyone would vote for this person being the better salesperson. But if that person is not asking enough closing questions in any given moment or not asking the right questions, that person will sell less than the salesperson who is less polished, less effective, and clearly not as good a salesperson, but who asks a greater number of well-chosen closing questions.

The person who is asking more closing questions is typically going to make more sales even if they are just prospecting and striving to set up opportunities for a closer. This is because opportunities are made stickier and are less likely to die between calls if conclusions are galvanized through appropriate closing questions during the prospecting stage.

So, pound for pound, I would argue that the way to galvanize people's closings is dependent on your ability to turn conversations into concluding moments by posing questions that force prospects to think things through. In the absence of putting all those ideas and techniques together in a way that creates the conclusion, a lot of the work that we're doing in pursuit of closing the sale gets lost and melts away.

Going back to the adage "always be closing," the question you really want to keep in mind throughout the pitch is "How am I going to lock in these conclusions in the prospect's mind?"

That's where we need to be to close the deal. Ask yourself the following questions:

- ❖ "How am I locking that in through my use of closing questions?"
- ❖ "How am I not allowing those conclusions to evaporate?"
- ❖ "What is the right level of specificity or directness needed at any given time between a trial close question that elicits feedback versus a direct closing question?"
- ❖ "Which kind of question is appropriate in many circumstances but not others?"

Then being able to make the most emotionally intelligent choices along the way as to what would be the right closing question, or the right degree of specificity in that closing question, or directness in that close, is typically where the practice of closing becomes an art and an instinct and even, to a large degree, predictable.

Those instincts are key to people knowing how to ask the perfect closing questions at the right moment, corresponding to where the prospect is. If they are in line with where the prospect is emotionally at any given time, that's where things resonate, like tuning a musical instrument. There's a huge correlation between the strength of the question and the resiliency of the conclusions by the prospect. Arguably, the magic lies in finding that perfect moment where the time of the question meets the space where the prospect is to create the reality of the artful close.

If people pay attention to this, they will understand closing in a more detailed way, and as a discipline on its own—because it *is* a discipline on its own. It is really the key to unlocking the benefits of all the other steps of the process that we've discussed. That's the magic of this. It's doing each and every one of these steps that we talked about at a performance level of either nine out of ten or ten out of ten that creates positive sales outcomes that are predictable. When we're executing these at the highest level, that's where we're the most efficient. That's where we're in a position to extract the maximum amount of success from the opportunities that we create.

Sales masters or people looking to master the art of sales will be attentive to these things. They're going to look humbly in the mirror and identify their weaknesses and turn those weaknesses into strengths through a systematic program of training and reviews, evaluation and reevaluation, and practice, practice. practice. There is a way to master sales, just like there is a way to master any sport, instrument, skill, or discipline.

Malcolm Gladwell talked about the ten-thousand-hour rule in his seminal book, *Outliers*. The book describes a University of Toronto study of NHL hockey players, which found that 40 percent of them were born between the months of January and March in their respective years. Such a trend is disproportionate compared to the expected 25 percent per quarter. In the end, it was not that some players in certain months were necessarily born to a higher degree with exceptional hockey talent. It mostly had to do with Canadian and other hockey associations' cut-off date, when younger players would cease to play with older kids at the end of the calendar year, eliminating that natural disadvantage.

This suggested that making the NHL was less about raw talent and more circumstantial about the level of adversity and the amount of practice and a variety of other primarily "nurture" based factors. Gladwell described how the Beatles became the biggest band in the world after practicing approximately ten hours a day for five years, and how Bill Gates became the wealthiest person in the world by practicing writing computer code for approximately ten thousand hours.

Though some critics argue this rule as described by Gladwell is oversimplified, because it focuses on the quantity of time practicing, not the quality of the practice, both factors combined absolutely do apply to sales. When I think back to when all the things that we're talking about became knowledge or second nature or instinct, I may not have put in ten thousand hours, but I had certainly put in a multitude of quality practice hours by then.

When I look at my best salespeople and my best closers, it's intuitive. I can listen to a live call and know exactly what they're going to say or what they're going to do, because the laws of sales that we talk about and the things to do at any given moment become so obvious.

It's not a crapshoot, it's not random—it's a process. And that process, applied perfectly, will create predictable results. If the process is pure, the outcomes are pure and predictable. That's what this book is all about.

WHAT TYPE OF SALESPERSON ARE YOU?

The "Big Tent" of Sales
Where are you on the continuum?

(Score yourself from 1-10)

<<Persuasive>>   <<Resistant>>

1	2-3	4-5	6-7	8-9	10
The customer is always right.	Customer service approach with some limits to avoid incentivizing customer complaints.	Nearly equal power dynamic between buyer and seller, but dropping the price and/or giving into other buyer requests is frequent.	Nearly equal power dynamic between buyer and seller, but dropping price is not an option. Staying firm on price to force a yes / no is likely. Adding some extra value to close is acceptable if high probability to resolve.	We are very selective when considering new clients, however with your credentials I'm quite sure you will qualify.	We are very selective, so why should we accept you as a new client? We will consider your application and get back to you as to whether or not you're approved.

For more insights and resources about optimizing sales strategies, visit geoffreymreid.com or by email at: geoffrey@geoffreymreid.com

WHAT TYPE OF SALESPERSON ARE YOU?

1. What is the most valuable characteristic of a salesperson?

A	B	C	D	E
Intelligence	Experience	Learning Style	Coachability	Attitude

2. Which sales training methods are considered most valuable for optimal employee development?

1. Classroom training sessions	4. Regular reviews followed by bespoke instruction
2. One-on-one training sessions	5. Tape training
3. Apprenticeship model with new hire watching others with experience	6. Strategy sessions with manager using live examples
7. All of the above	

3. Which two (2) answers below best describe how to most effectively prospect new customers:

1. Cold calling	4. Other communication mediums: Whatsapp Telegram; Text; Signal
2. Email prospecting	5. Other social media (ie. Facebook, Instagram, Tiktok, X)
3. LinkedIn	6. All of the above

For more insights and resources about optimizing sales strategies, visit geoffreymreid.com or by email at: geoffrey@geoffreymreid.com

WHAT TYPE OF SALESPERSON ARE YOU?

4. Name five (5) sales process tools most commonly used by salespeople

1	
2	
3	
4	
5	

5. Name four (4) most common types of closing questions:

1	
2	
3	
4	

To continue, scan the QR code below to access this interactive knowledge check.

For more insights and resources about optimizing sales strategies, visit geoffreymreid.com or by email at: geoffrey@geoffreymreid.com

Geoffrey M. Reid
CEO | Consultant | Professor

Geoffrey Reid began his career over thirty years ago as a public policy analyst in the Canadian Public Service after completing an undergraduate degree from Bishop's University. In recent years, he has been serving as a CEO for a private multinational company with fifty locations around the world and is a global leader in business events and sales.

Photo Credit: Petruta Moldovan

In between, Geoffrey added a master's degree, pursued doctoral studies, and worked as a self-employed mediator, trainer, and consultant for both public and private sector clients. In the five years that preceded his career shift to sales, Geoffrey also worked as an adjunct professor with the School of Graduate Studies at Concordia University in Montreal, Canada, teaching negotiation, mediation, and conflict resolution at the master's level.

Geoffrey began his sales career in Montreal in the year 2000 in junior sales position, with the primary objective of learning sales—something he knew nothing about at the time. At the end of his first full year in sales, Geoffrey had generated more new personal sales revenue than any other employee in North America. Shortly thereafter, he entered management, and rose through the ranks to take local then national responsibility for all offices in Canada.

In 2014, he was given international responsibilities and moved to global headquarters in London, UK, to accept a chief executive officer position, taking approximately one hundred flights per year to support offices in Asia, Europe, and North America.

His most satisfying contribution is having hired and/or developed, directly or indirectly, many of the current top sales performers, managers, and directors. Much of this satisfaction comes from Geoffrey having had the opportunity to share skill sets that have allowed his employees to generate top-end incomes for their own benefit and that of their families.

Since the pandemic, Geoffrey has returned home to Montreal to play similar roles. He is now traveling less and using Zoom more. This has allowed him more time to share more broadly what he has learned in his quarter-century sales career to help make up for the lack of sales education that exists in most business schools and elsewhere.

www.ingramcontent.com/pod-product-compliance
Lightning Source LLC
Chambersburg PA
CBHW030505210326
41597CB00013B/799